Memoirs of the Royal Artillery Band

...ND

...u teholier ...

...ITH 14 ...

1. ...

...Y & CO., ...REET
AND

ROYAL ARTILLERY BAND, WOOLWICH, 1901.

MEMOIRS

OF THE

ROYAL ARTILLERY BAND

ITS ORIGIN, HISTORY AND PROGRESS

An Account of the Rise of Military Music in England

BY

HENRY GEORGE FARMER

Bombardier, Royal Artillery Band

".... I am beholden to you for your sweet music"
—PERICLES

WITH 14 ILLUSTRATIONS

LONDON
BOOSEY & CO., 295, REGENT STREET
AND NEW YORK
1904

TO THE OFFICERS

OF THE

ROYAL REGIMENT OF ARTILLERY

THIS HISTORY

OF THEIR REGIMENTAL BAND

IS

BY PERMISSION

MOST RESPECTFULLY DEDICATED.

PREFACE.

" Now, instead of going on denying that we are an
unmusical nation, let us do our utmost to prove that we
are a musical nation."—SIR ALEX. MACKENZIE.

" A HISTORY of British Military Music is much needed."
So said the *Musical Times* some six or seven years ago;
and to-day, when military music and military bands are so
much discussed, a work of this kind appears to be urgently
called for.

This volume, however, makes no pretence whatever to
supply the want, but merely claims to be a history of *one* of
the famous bands in the service, that of the Royal Artillery.
The records of this band date as far back as 1762, when it
was formed, and I doubt if there is another band in the
army with a continuous history for so long a period. It
was the first regimental band to be officially recognised and
provided for in the Army Estimates, and may therefore
justly claim to be the pioneer band of the British Army,
whilst its history may fairly be stated to represent the
growth of the military band in this country.

I desire to tender my thanks to all those who have so
readily responded to my enquiries, several of whom I have
acknowledged in the body of the work; but more especially
have I to acknowledge the services of three old members
of the band—the late James Lawson, Esq. (bandmaster,
R.A. Mounted Band), Joseph Smith, Esq., and W. F. Howe,
Esq., for their untiring efforts to make these memoirs as
complete as possible.

To the Superintendent of the R.A. Record Office—
R. C. W. Williams, Esq., R.A., I respectfully beg to
acknowledge my indebtedness for his courtesy in permitting

me to have access to the regimental records. I have also to thank C.-S.-Major A. W. H. Seville, R.A., of that office, for his kind assistance.

Major R. H. Murdoch, late R.A.—late Superintendent of the R.A. Record Office; R. J. Jackson, Esq.—Editor of the *Kentish Independent*; and W. T. Vincent, Esq.—President of the Woolwich Antiquarian Society, and author of the *Records of Woolwich*; have all most kindly given me information, for which I beg leave to tender my most cordial thanks.

But above all these, I have to express my deepest gratitude to the Editor of the *Orchestral Times*—James A. Browne, Esq., the author of *England's Artillerymen*, which work formed the nucleus of these memoirs. This gentleman most generously placed his services at my disposal, and not only have I had the benefit of his invaluable collection of notes and papers relating to artillery history and military music, but I feel that I can never sufficiently thank him for his great interest, encouragement, and excellent advice, to which is due in no small way any success which this little volume may attain.

The four plates, showing the dress worn by the band at various periods, are from the pen of a talented member of the band—Frank Ashton, to whom I am extremely grateful for the great care and attention which he gave to ensure absolute accuracy in the matter of dress.

In placing this work before the regiment and public generally, it is with the hope that they may consider the matter worthy of the time and labour bestowed upon it. With the members and ex-members of the R.A. Band who have so enthusiastically supported its publication, it may be the means of furthering that *esprit de corps* which has always been so highly maintained among them, and I trust that they may derive as much pleasure in reading of their worthy ancestors as I have done in unearthing their history.

H. G. F.

R.A. BAND, WOOLWICH,
June, 1904.

CONTENTS.

List of Illustrations.

INTRODUCTION.

"What passion cannot music raise and quell."—DRYDEN.

"Music the fiercest grief can charm,
"And Fate's severest rage disarm."—POPE.

*M*USIC is an essential to war, and an army would as soon think of leaving its gunpowder as its harmony at home. In all nations from the earliest times music has been the accompaniment of feats of arms, and served the two-fold purpose of inspiring the troops to fight, and as a means of conveying orders or commands. The noisiest instruments were naturally the best adapted for this purpose :—

"The shrill trump,[1] the spirit-stirring drum."
—SHAKESPEARE.

and with no less policy do those act who trust to their efficacy in the hour of battle, and use them as a means of exciting that passion which the most eloquent oration imaginable would fail to inspire.

[1] BARTHOLOMÆUS, who wrote *De Proprietatibus Rerum* about 1366, says :—
"A trompe is properly an instrument ordeyned for men that fyghteth in batayle, to crye and to warne of the sygnes of batayle. . . Men in olde tyme usyd trompes in battayle to fere and affraye theyr enmyes, and to comforte theyre owne knyghtes and fyghtynge men. . . . For it is somtime blowe to arraye battaylles, and somtyme for that bataylles sholde smyte togyder." (Published by Stephen Batman in 1582.)

B

Both of these instruments are of the most remote antiquity. The Ethiopians attribute to the Egyptian god Thoth the introduction of the drum into their country in the first year of the creation of the world. But it is more probable that it was transmitted from the Ethiopians to the Egyptians, for it is historically affirmed that the latter originally migrated from Ethiopia.

Some Greek historians credit the Tyrrhenians[1] with the invention of the trumpet, to direct their soldiers in time of war, and to supersede lighted torches and shells of fishes, which were sounded like trumpets. But others, with greater probability, ascribe it to the Egyptians. Martial music had its place with the Egyptians, as with all nations of antiquity, but with them it was almost entirely confined to the use of trumpets and drums.[2] These trumpets were straight, and, according to Sir J. Gardner Wilkinson, eighteen inches in length. They also used an instrument called the *sistrum*, which, according to Batman, before quoted, was "like a horn, used in battaile insteed of a trumpet."

The trumpets used by the Hebrews during their forty years sojourn in the wilderness were doubtless of Egyptian origin. Moses, as the disciple of Egyptian priests, was intimately acquainted with the practice of music. He was commanded to make "two trumpets of silver." (Numbers x.) These trumpets, called by the Jews *chatzozerah*, are the only Jewish instruments of which any

[1] VIRGIL calls it the Tyrrhenian trumpet.
[2] *History of Music.*—NAUMANN.

authentic representation exists. They appear in
the celebrated bas-relief on the Arch of Titus at
Rome. A portion of the mosaic ordinances is
devoted to the use of these trumpets. The tribes
were gathered together by the blowing of trumpets,
and in the 9th verse of Numbers x. we find :—

> "And if ye go to war in your land against
> the enemy that oppresseth you, then ye shall
> blow an alarm with the trumpets."

Josephus says that they were a little less than
a cubit in length, but, from the representation,
they would appear to have been longer. The horn
(*shophar* and *keren*) was also a warlike instrument
with them ; for Josephus says that the soldiers of
Gideon used it.

Music was held in the highest estimation among
the Greeks during the whole period of their history.
The trumpet was not in use with them during the
Trojan war, although it was quite common in the
time of Homer.[1] The celebrated Athenian general,
Tyrtæus, who lived six centuries before Christ, was
an excellent performer upon the trumpet, and it
was he who first induced the Spartans to employ it
as a military instrument, during the wars with the
Messenians. It seems that the most important
martial instruments of the Greeks were the

---

[1] Sir James Turner (*Pallas Armata*) explains how the
Greeks got the trumpet. He says they learned the use
of it from the Tyrrhenians, and they, having their name
and origin from the Tirians, had their trumpets also from
them. The Tirians being neighbours of the Jews, learned
many things from them, and probably the trumpet. Thus
we see how the trumpet was transmitted from Egypt into
Europe.

straight trumpet—*salphinx*, the small trumpet with
a curvature towards the bell, and the horn—*keras*.
Every company of infantry had a trumpeter; and
in the cavalry also, although not mentioned by
Ælian, there appears to have been a trumpeter,
or horn-player.

The Romans had, no doubt, a national music
peculiar to themselves, but music as an art they
borrowed, as they did every other artistic adjunct
of their national life, from the Greeks. The
Romans were a race of fighting men, and regarded
military music more seriously than any other
branch of the art. It was King Servius Tullius
who introduced into the Roman army trumpets
and horns of metal, in the year 570 B.C. In later
years, however, we find quite a host of martial
instruments, the most important of which were
the straight trumpet—*tuba*[1]; the huge curved
trumpet—*buccina*; the small trumpet—*lituus*;
and the horn—*cornu*.[2] The performers on these
instruments were called Æneatores. Every troop
of horse, and every maniple, if not every century
of foot, had either a trumpet or horn, or both.[3]

The *tuba* was employed for signals of every
description in war, and Vegetius says that the
signal for the advance and retire was sounded
upon it, as was also the fanfare at the sacrifice
celebrated in the presence of the army. The

[1] The *tuba* is usually designated as being about 39 inches
long. There are several specimens in the British Museum.

[2] The *cornu* in the British Museum measures 4 feet
6 inches in length.

[3] *Pallas Armata*—TURNER, 1683.

guards and sentries were posted to the sound of the *tuba*, and relieved by the sounding of the *cornu*. The signal for the starting of the army was given on this instrument, and probably a marching tune was played on it ; *cornicines* at least walk in front of the marching army[1] on the Column of Antonius and the Arch of Constantine.[2] The purpose of the *buccina*, which was an enormous instrument, the tube measuring fully eleven feet in length, was to direct the movements of troops detached from camp.[3] The *lituus* probably served the same purpose as the *tuba*, the former being allotted to the cavalry, and the latter to the infantry.[4]

But there can be no doubt that *our* pagan forefathers used neither trumpet nor bugle when preparing for the fray, but the more uncouth buffalo horn. Cæsar himself writes that the aboriginal inhabitants of our island, the Ancient Britons, were passionately fond of music, both instrumental and vocal. Their music, like their national character, was sensitive, impetuous, ardent, and at times imbued with a wild melancholy and deep pathos. It is said to have been so extremely

---

[1] Marèchal de Saxe in his *Rèveries* gives as one reason the Romans were generally victorious that they were made to march in time. "This is the perfect secret, the military step of the Romans. It is the reason of the institution of marches and the beating of the drum."

[2] *Life of the Greeks and Romans.*—GUHL & KONER, 1877.

[3] *History of Music.*—NAUMANN.

[4] This does not seem to have always been the rule. Ovid mentions that the infantry of the Sabines and Romans used the *lituus*, and we find that the cavalry used both the *tuba* and *buccina.*—*Dictionary of Greek and Roman Antiquities.* —W. SMITH, 1891.

affecting that sometimes when two armies were standing in the order of battle, and on the point of engaging in the most furious combat, the bards would step between them and by their soft, fascinating strains, calm the fury of the warriors, and so prevent bloodshed.[1]

The Ancient Britons were in the habit of using horns to increase the din of battle. We are told that they began their attacks with taunting songs and deafening howls, accompanied by the blowing of horns, with which each warrior was provided. Several instruments of the horn species have been discovered in Ireland, a country rich in Celtic antiquities, and are considered by many writers to be Celtic, although several have assigned them to the Danes.[2] There is a record of ten or twelve being discovered in the bogs of County Cork. Several specimens are preserved at the Royal Irish Academy at Dublin, and are of considerable size, having the embouchere at the side, like an Ashantee war-trumpet.

The horn was also a martial instrument with the Saxons. There is a drawing in the manuscript of Prudentius, which seems to represent a sort of military dance or sham combat. There are two men, equipped in martial habits, armed with sword and shield, engaged in combat to the music of the horn.[3]

The reference to the war-horn in the poem

[1] *History of Music.*—STAFFORD, 1838.
[2] *Irish Antiquities.*—WAKEMAN, 1847.
[3] *Sport and Pastimes.*—STRUTT, 1833.

Beowulf is sufficient evidence that it was a martial instrument with them in the fifth century :—

> "They away hurried bitter and angry
> The instant they heard the war-horn sing."

It is mentioned also in later Anglo-Saxon glossaries, so that we may come to the conclusion that although Tacitus tells us that they marched to battle to the sound of their own voices, yet they were collected in the first instance by the sound of the horn.[1]

"Besides the horn," says Strutt,[2] "they had a long trumpet," which, in the manuscript given by him, is slightly curved and of great size, being fully five feet in length. On the side of the manuscript is inscribed :—

> "When the trumpet ceases to sound, the
> sword is returned to the scabbard."

With the Danes, also, "the call to arms was by the sound of the trumpet, or horn."

In the *History of Charles and Grymer, Swedish Kings,* Harec, hearing of his son's death, cries out :—

> "Let the bugle-horn sound to arms, I will
> go and ravage Sweden."

In the same history we find: "All instantly fly to arms, and everyone prepares himself for battle; the trumpet sounds, and each warrior is accoutred." Several trumpets have been found in Britain, and

---

[1] *Older England.*—HODGETTS, 1884.

[2] *Manners, Customs, etc., of England.*—STRUTT, 1775.

are generally supposed to have been Danish.[1]

The science of music suffered nothing in England
from the Norman invasion. Their martial music
was much upon the same plan as that of the
Saxons.[2] When William the Conqueror sailed
from the Dive for the shores of England, we are
told that his ships "resounded with music; the
pipe, the zittern, the drums, the cymbals, all were
heard, and the voice of the trumpet sounded
proudly over all."[3] His army was accompanied by
minstrels, one of whom, named Taillefer, having
obtained leave to begin the onset, advanced at the
head of the army, singing with a loud voice the
songs which immortalised the valour of Roland and
Charlemagne, and as he sang he performed feats
with his sword. The Normans repeated the burden
of the song, with shouts of " Dieu Aide !" Taillefer
was killed in the struggle. In the several poetical
narratives of the battle of Hastings there is frequent
mention of trumpets and horns :—

> " Dez ki li dous ost s'entrevirent."
> " Grant noise é grant temulte firent."
> " Mult oïssiez graisles soner."
> " E *boisines é cors* corner."
> —ROMAN DE ROU.

Military music did not assume any definite shape
until the time of the Crusades. The returning
Crusaders brought with them many new customs

---

[1] *Military Antiquities*—GROSE, 1801—in which there is
an engraving of a Danish trumpet, over five feet in length.

[2] *Manners, Customs, etc., of England.*—STRUTT, 1775.

[3] *History of the Norman Conquest.*—FREEMAN, 1869.

from the East, and they are credited with the introduction of drums and kettledrums into our armies.[1] These instruments are frequently mentioned in the accounts of the Crusades. The side drum[2] (*tabour*[3]) is introduced into the romance of Richard Cœur de Lion[4]:—

"Tambours beten and trumpes blowe."

The kettledrums (*nakeres*[5]) occur in the *Memoirs of St. Louis* (JOINVILLE), where we are told that the tumult and noise made by the Saracens with their horns and *nacaires* was frightful to hear, and seemed very strange to the French.

In the Saracen armies, trumpets and drums were used to indicate a rallying point; for although at ordinary times the standards sufficed to show men the places of their leaders, yet in the dust of battle these were often hidden from sight; and it was therefore the rule to gather the minstrels around the standards, and bid them blow and beat strenuously and unceasingly during the action. The silence of the band was taken as a proof that a battalion had been broken, and that the colours were in danger; and the fashion lasted so long that even in the seventeenth century the bandsmen in all battle pictures are depicted, drawn up at a safe distance, energetically playing.[6]

[1] *History of Music.*—NAUMANN.

[2] Drum, from the Erse, Drumme.

[3] *Tabour* (English), *Tambour* (French).

[4] *History of English Poetry.*—WARTON, 1824.

[5] *Nakeres* (English), *nacaires* (French), *nacchera* (Italian), from the *nagarah* of the Arabs and Moors.

[6] *History of the British Army.*—FORTESCUE, 1899.

For the next two hundred years at least the instrument used for signalling appears to have been the trumpet alone,[1] although so far as can be gathered it sounded no distinct calls, but was dependent for its significance on orders previously issued. (The signals for the horn in the chase were, however, numerous.) Froissart informs us that orders were made known by the trumpet :—
" Au premier son de sa trompette ou s'appareillât, au second on s'armât, et aut tiers son montât à cheval et partit."

After the Norman Conquest the itinerant professors of music became known as minstrels. The king and nobility had their minstrels, who held important ranks in the court of the Norman monarchs. When they took command of their armies in the field of war, they were accompanied by their minstrels, both for signalling and for enlivening the dreariness of the camp or march.[2] In the public expenditures made in the fifth year of Edward I. (1276) there is payment to one named Robert, styled " King of the Minstrels," being chief of them apparently for military service[3];

[1] *Dictionary of Music and Musicians.*—GROVE.

It is in Italy that the side drum seems first to have been used for this purpose. Macchiavelli, in his *Art of War* (1521) clearly states that the drum commands all things in a battle, proclaiming the commands of the officer to his troops. It was from Italy that in all probability the earliest musical signals came : spread over Europe by mercenaries, they were modified and altered by the different troops which adopted them : but the names given to the different sounds long retained evidence of their Italian origin.

[2] *Military Music* —KAPPEY.

[3] *History of the British Army.*—SCOTT, 1868.

and in 1293 there is a payment to Randolph, the King's Trumpeter, who had also been trumpeter to Henry III. In the fourth year of Edward II. (1310) there is a charge for Janino la Chevretter (bagpiper), Roger the Trumpeter, and Janino le Nakerer (kettledrummer), all of them King's Minstrels, who received sixty shillings from the king. The court minstrels of Edward III. consisted of: 5 trompetters, 2 clarions,[1] 5 pypers, 3 wayghtes,[2] and four others,[3] who held fine positions, each being paid 7½d. daily, "by letters patent," to be received at the exchequer during his life; besides other rewards, such as in 1359, when forty pounds were given to the king's herald and his companions the minstrels for attending the tournament at Smithfield.[4]

There is a ballad (Harleian MS.) made on the victory of Edward III. over the Scots at Hallidon Hill (1333) :—

> "This was do with merry sowne
> With pipes, Trompes and Tabers therto
> And loude clarionnes thei blew also."

and in the prose account to be found in the same manuscript :—

> "Then the Engliche mynstrelles beten ther tabers, and blewen their Trompes, and pipers pipedene loude and made a grete schowte upon the Skottes."

---

[1] Clarion—a small trumpet.

[2] Wayghts or Waits—an ancient wooden instrument played with a double reed; the precursor of the oboe.

[3] *History of Music.*—HAWKINS, 1776.

[4] *Issue Roll of Thomas de Brantingham.*—A.D. 1370.

Froissart describes how, in the year 1347, when Edward III. and his queen made their triumphal entry into Calais, they were greeted with a grand military concert of "trompes, de tambours, de nacaires, de chalemies[1] et de muses." That these were instruments of martial music there can be no doubt, for Chaucer, in his description of the tournament in the *Knight's Tale*, says:—

> " Pipes, trompes, nakeres, and clariounes
> That in the bataille blowen blody sounes."

He also informs us that the archer of this period was furnished with a horn :—

> " An horn he bare, his baudrik was of grene."

Among the court minstrels of the good King " Hal " we find one named John Cliff and seventeen others, ten of whom were clarion players, and were paid twelvepence each per diem. They accompanied the king on his expedition to Harfleur in 1415, and served at Guienne and elsewhere.

This John Cliff was one of the court minstrels with Henry VI. when he and others were empowered to impress minstrels into the king's service.[2]

One of this name also appears among the thirteen minstrels of Edward IV. (1470), " whereof some be trompets, some with the shalmes and small pypes."[3] They were paid and clothed by the king, besides other rewards from the exchequer ;

---

[1] Chalemie or chalemeau (French), shalm or shawm (English), was the precursor of the clarionet.

[2] Rymer's *Fœdera*.

[3] *History of Music.*—Hawkins.

and received nightly " four gallons of ale," together with fuel, light and lodging for themselves and their horses. Two servants were also allowed them " to bear their trompets, pypes and other instruments."

As they served on horseback, the custom arose of looking upon trumpet music as being specially appropriate for the cavalry service,[1] whilst in the " bands" of foot the tabour, or side drum, was used, and frequently in conjunction with the bagpipe.[2] The latter was a decided favourite in England, being used on all public occasions, and very popular with troops raised in Ireland and in the north.[3]

There exists a curious and most remarkable piece of music, by William Byrd, composed somewhere about the end of the sixteenth century, entitled *The Battell*, in which is to be found " The Souldiers' Summons," " The Martch of Ffoote," " The Martch of Horse," " The Irish Martch," " The Trumpetts," " The Bagpipe and the Drum," etc. They are most probably old and familiar marches.

[1] The trumpet retained its original straight form until the sixteenth century, which is proved by a picture that hangs in Windsor Castle representing the interview between Henry VIII. and Francis I. in 1520. The credit of having bent the tube of the trumpet is usually claimed for a Frenchman named Maurin (1498-1515), but the transformation really took place in Italy about the middle of the thirteenth century.

[2] Bartholomæus, who wrote about 1366, says that the *tympanum* " maketh better melody yf there is a pype therewyth."

[3] The bagpipe is mentioned by Procopius as an instrument of war with the Roman infantry.

During the reign of Henry VIII. the fife appears
as a martial instrument in England, and in time
became so popular as to almost oust the bagpipe
from its position as an accompaniment to the drum.
Grose, in his *Military Antiquities* (1801), says that
the fife is a German invention introduced into
military music by the Swiss.[1] In an "Ordonnance"
of Francis I. of France, in 1534, each band of
1,000 men, was to have four tabourins and two fifes
(*Memoirs de Du Bellay*), and therefore, according to
precedent, we may infer that it was introduced
shortly afterwards into the British service. We
find it first in the muster of the citizens of London
in 1539, when "droumes" and "ffyffers" are
mentioned.

Henry VIII. evidently took some interest in this
class of music, for it is recorded that he sent all the
way to Vienna to procure kettledrums that could
be played on horseback "after the Hungarian (that
is to say the hussars) manner," together with men
that could make and play them skilfully. Ten good
drums and as many fifers were ordered at the same
time.

The employment of fifes in our armies was the
first step towards the formation of the military
band.

---

[1] Mersenne (*Harmonie Universelle*—1639) calls it *tibia
helvetica*, and says it is the same species as the flute, but
proportionately less in every respect, wherefore it sounds
more acutely and vehemently, which it ought to do, lest the
sound of it should be drowned by that of the drum.

CHAPTER I.

1557-1762.

" Nothing is more apt, than music to raise man to great deeds, and chiefly to inspire him with the degree of courage necessary to brave the dangers of war."—PLUTARCH.

" The sound of trumpet and of drum,
That makes the warrior's stomach come ;
Whose noise whets valour sharp, like beer
By thunder turned to vinegar ;
(For if you hear a trumpet sound or drum beat
Who has not a month's mind to combat ?)"
—BUTLER'S " HUDIBRAS."

THE earliest mention of " music " or " musician " in the Royal Artillery is given in the list of the army despatched to St. Quentin, 1557, where a " drumme " and " phife " are employed at one shilling each per diem, for the " Trayne of Artillery."

These drum and fife bands were but poor affairs of a very dull kind. The manipulation of the fife was very rudimentary, and the side drums, instead of being short, having a bright and powerful tone, which is greatly increased by the addition of snares over the lower head, were twice as long as the modern ones, had no snares,[1] and the shell was made of wood.

---

[1] So says Kappey (*Military Music*). But in the work of Michael Pretorius (*Syntagma Musicum*—1619) the side drum is distinctly shown with snares.

There are rules laid down for drummers and fifers of this period by one Ralph Smith :—" All capitaines must have drommes and ffifes and men to use the same, whoe shall be faithfull, secrette, and ingenious, of able personage to use their instruments and office, of sundrie languages ; for oftentimes they bee sent to parley with their enemies, to sommon theire efforts and dyverse other messages, which of necessitie requireth language. If such drommes and ffifes should fortune to fall into the hands of the enemies, noe guifte nor force should cause them to disclose any secrettes that they knowe. They must ofte practice theire instruments, teach the companye the soundes of the marche, allarum, approache, assaulte, battaile, retreate, skirmishe, or any other callinge that of necessitie should be knowen. They must be obediente to the commandemente of theire captaine and ensigne, when as they shall command them to comme, goe, or stande, or sounde theire retreate or callinge."

For all these requirements and accomplishments they received the munificent reward of one shilling per diem, which was fourpence more than the common soldier received. Indeed, if they did a tithe of that which was expected of them, they were worth every penny of it. Trumpeters of horse were required to know six calls : " Saddle !" " Mount !" " Mess !" " March !" " Alarm !" and " Charge !"[1]

---

[1] *History of the British Army*—FORTESCUE, 1899.

In the train of artillery raised in 1620, for the recovery of the Palatinate, a trumpeter and drummer are employed at two shillings and one shilling per diem respectively. But in the "train" commissioned in 1639 for service in Scotland they are omitted, although other branches had them. Trumpeters of "horse" two shillings and sixpence per diem, and drummers of "foot" one shilling per diem. However, the artillery train of 1685 has a drummer at one shilling, and three years later two are allowed at one shilling and sixpence per diem.

Trumpeters and drummers were furnished for the army by the Sergeant-Trumpeter and the Drum-Major-General[1] of the Royal Household, whose duty it was to impress musicians for the service.[2] They also granted licences to other than King's troops wishing to sound a trumpet or beat a drum. Impressing musicians seems to have been anything but a pleasant duty; for we find that in the year 1637, the Sergeant-Trumpeter appointed Cuthbert Collins, a "Trumpeter in Ordinary," to impress one John Digges, when the latter challenged him to fight and otherwise abused him.

All this was many years before the "Royal Regiment of Artillery" was established; and in these pre-regimental days the Master-General of Ordnance was responsible for the raising of the trains of artillery, of which he was *ex-officio* colonel-

---

[1] These offices first appear in the reign of Edward VI., when Benedict Browne was Sergeant-Trumpeter, and Robert Bruer was "Master Drummer."

[2] In 1679, there is a payment of five pounds twelve shillings made to Drum-Major-General Mawgridge, for impressing sixteen drummers for the Coldstream Guards.

in-chief. Not only did he control this department, but he directed the Board of Ordnance,
which included everything pertaining to ordnance
and military stores. When the Master-General
took to the field in time of war, we find among
his staff or retinue, a trumpeter and kettledrummer.
The kettledrums were mounted on a chariot drawn
by six white horses.[1] They appear in the field for
the first time during the Irish Rebellion of 1689,
and the estimates for ordnance, &c., includes " large
kettledrums mounted on a carriage with cloaths
marked I.R. (Jacobus Rex), and cost £158 9s."[2]

The kettledrummer, whose name was John Bur-
nett, held a fine position, being paid four shillings per
diem, and his uniform cost fifty pounds. Even the
driver of the kettledrums received three shillings per
diem, and could not be clothed under fifteen pounds,
while a gunner's suit was valued at five pounds
six shillings and fourpence. These kettledrums
were peculiar only to the artillery. The cavalry
kettledrums, although mentioned in the reign of
Henry VIII., were not universally acknowledged
until James II. came to the throne. Sir James
Turner, who wrote *Pallas Armata* (1683), speaks
of them as being quite a novelty:—" There is,"
he says, " another martial instrument used with the
cavalry, which they call the kettledrum; there be
two of them, which hang before the drummer's
saddle, on both which he beats. They are not
ordinary; princes, dukes and earls may have them

---

[1] *History of the R.A.*—DUNCAN.
[2] *Artillery Regimental History.*—MILLER.

with the troops which ordinarily are called life
guards. So may generals and lieutenant-generals,
though they be not noblemen. The Germans,
Danes and Swedes permit none under a baron to
have them unless they are taken in battle from an
enemy."[1]

Manesson Mallet says :—" The timbal player
should be a man of heart, preferring rather to
perish in the combat than to allow himself to be
taken with his drums. He should have a pleasing
motion of the arm, an accurate ear, and take
delight in diverting his master by agreeable airs
in deeds of mirth."[2]

It has already been shown how the fife came
into such favour, as to entirely supersede the
bagpipe, except perhaps in the north, where it
continues a favourite to the present day. Sir
James Turner (1683) says :—" In some places a
Piper is allowed to each company : the Germans
have him, and I look upon their Pipe as a Warlike

---

[1] A similar rule was observed in England. At the
Restoration, no regiment of horse was permitted to use
kettledrums. The only regiment that had them was the
Life Guards. However, on the accession of James II.,
every regiment of horse was furnished with them. At the
latter part of the eighteenth century there were only two
regiments in the service, besides the Life Guards and Horse
Guards, who were allowed to employ them : the Royal
Irish Dragoons and the King's Dragoons (3rd Hussars), by
virtue of having captured them from an enemy ; the former
at Hockstedt, 1704, and the latter at Dettingen, 1743.
Why these regiments should have been specially favoured
is not quite clear, for similar trophies were in the possession
of other regiments. The 3rd Dragoon Guards captured
the drums of the Bavarian Guards at Ramilies, 1706, and
the 7th Dragoon Guards captured a pair from the French
at Dettingen, 1743.

[2] Paris, 1683.

Instrument. The Bagpipe is good enough musick for them who love it, but sure it is not so good as the Almain whistle [fife]. With us any Captain may keep a piper in his company and maintain him too, for no pay is allowed him, perhaps just as much as he deserveth."

Even the fife did not receive universal acceptance. Francis Markham, in his *Five Decades of Epistles of Warre* (1622), seems to have been somewhat opposed to its use, for in action the soldier was likely to have his attention diverted from the drum signals by the music of the fifes. He says :—" It is to the voice of the Drum the Souldier should wholly attend, and not to the aire of a whistle." Shakespeare, whose eye and ear escaped nothing, refers to the " ear-piercing fife," and in the *Merchant of Venice* he has a word for " the vile squealing of the wry-neck'd fife."

In turn, the fife suffered the same fate as the bagpipe ; perhaps even worse, for it appears for a time to have been banished altogether from our service. It appears for the last time in the Coronation Procession of James II. In Sandford's picture of that event, a fifer is shown (having a banner attached to his fife) dressed in the king's livery, marching in front of the four drummers of the Guards,[1] dressed in a like manner.

The instrument that in all probability caused the abandonment of the fife was the hautboy. It is said by Mersenne, a learned French philosopher,

---

[1] In the *Souldier's Accidence* (1643) it says :—" The phipher (if there be more than one) the eldest, shall march with the eldest drumme."

who was the author of *Harmonie Universelle* (1636),
to be a French invention, and shown by him in
three forms—the treble, tenor, and bass. In France
it was customary to attach two hautbois and two
drums to each company.[1] We notice it first in our
service in 1678, in which year the Horse Grenadier
Guards were raised, each troop employing two
hautboys.

One of the last acts performed by Charles II. concerning the army is a warrant dated January 3rd,
1684-5, authorising the entertainment of twelve
hautbois in the companies of the King's Regiment
of Foot Guards in London, and that a fictitious
name should be borne on the strength of each of
the other companies of the regiment quartered in
the country, with a view to granting these musicians
a higher rate of pay.[2] The introduction of the
hautboy was a further advance towards the military
band. That they played in parts is evident from
the "music of the Grenadier Company" of the
Honourable Artillery Company, which in 1731
consisted of "one curtail, three hautbois, and no
more." So popular did the instrument become

---

[1] Charles II. of England copied many of his court
manners and customs from the French. He introduced
a court band of "24 violins," after the manner of the
French king's "Vingt-quarte Violons du Roi." So that it
is quite likely that the introduction of the hautboy into our
army came also from the French. The French word
"bande" was applied to the "Violons du Roi" of Louis XIV.,
so we may infer that Charles borrowed the term "bande"
when he introduced his "Violins." The word first appears
in a MS. order in the Lord Chamberlain's Warrant Books
for 1661. The old English word for a combination of
musical instruments in performance, was "noise."

[2] *History of the Grenadier Guards.*—HAMILTON 1874.

that it was generally adopted by regiments of dragoons and foot.[1]

Strange to say, it never found its way into the "Trains of Artillery." They still continued to employ the "Great Kettledrums" which accompanied the Duke of Marlborough to Holland in 1702, and formed a conspicuous feature at his funeral. A model of these drums and their carriage is preserved in the Rotunda Museum at Woolwich, and the silk and gold embossed bannerols are to be seen in the hall of the Ordnance Office, Royal Arsenal.

On the 26th May, 1716, the "Royal Regiment of Artillery" was formed; when two companies were permanently established at Woolwich. No drummers or other musicians are shown upon the establishment, although they appear in the "train" of 1715, and the Vigo expedition of 1719. But in 1720, His Majesty George I. was pleased to authorise an alteration in the establishment of the two companies, and we find two drummers at one shilling each per diem attached to each company.[2]

[1] "The dragoons long had the Haubois and side drum," says Grose (*Mil. Antiq.*, 1801), "but about the year 1759 changed them for the trumpet." Grose is evidently mistaken on this point. It was in 1764 that His Majesty George III. thought proper to forbid the use of brass side drums in the light cavalry. Lieut.-Col. Dalrymple, of the King's Own Dragoons, wrote an essay on the merits of both instruments, and it is not improbable that this assisted in its abolition (*Story of the 17th Lancers*— PARRY). It was not dispensed with at once, for we find that both the 3rd Dragoon Guards (*Cannon's Records*) and the 3rd Light Dragoons (*Records of the 3rd Light Dragoons*—KAUNTZE) did not adopt trumpets until 1766. The hautbois continued in favour some little time afterwards, and was retained in the Guards longer than any other corps.

[2] *Early History of the R.A.*—CLEAVELAND.

THE GREAT KETTLEDRUMS, TRAIN OF ARTILLERY.

THE GREAT KETTLEDRUMS, TRAIN OF ARTILLERY,

1702

The first drummer enlisted was Joseph Brome, aged eight years,[1] who, however, first appears upon the pay lists of 1721. These drummers were clothed in scarlet, a privilege extended to Royal regiments only.[2]

Joseph Brome died in 1796 a lieutenant-general, and had been three times Commandant of Woolwich garrison. There is an anecdote related of him in Browne's *England's Artillerymen*:—" On one occasion, while he was Commandant, he was entering the Warren (now the Royal Arsenal) when the guard turned out, presented arms, and the drummer beat two ruffles; little Brome ran up in great displeasure to the drummer, and upbraiding him for his inefficiency in the art of drumming, snatched the drum away, passed the suspending belt over his own neck,[3] and began to rattle away in a very superior style. Finishing with the two ruffles, he exclaimed: ' There, you young dog, that's the way I used to beat the drum when I was a drummer.' "

The kettledrummer continued to be borne on the staff of the regiment,[4] and accompanied the " train " in the Vigo expedition of 1719. These kettledrums appear in the field for the last time during the Flanders campaign, which terminated in 1748.[5] On

---

[1] This is not, however, an early age for the R.A. Most probably the youngest soldier to be borne on the pay lists of the regiment was Joseph Elliot, who was enlisted in 1804, when only four years old.

[2] *The Brome Family.*—MURDOCH.

[3] In the old days, drummers wore the drum sling round their necks, not over their shoulder as to-day.

[4] *History of the R.A.*—DUNCAN, 1872.

[5] *Artillery Regimental History.*—MILLER.

this occasion they were mounted on a triumphal car, finely ornamented and gilt, and drawn by six white horses.[1] On the fore part of the car was carried the Ordnance flag.[2] The position of the kettledrums on the march was in front of the flag-gun, and behind the Artillery front-guard[3]; when in camp they were placed in front of the quarters of the Duke of Cumberland, and the Artillery guns parked round them.[4] A regimental order of the 19th June, 1747, Herenthout, directs the kettle-drummer "to mount the kettledrum carriage every night half an hour before the sun sett, and beat till gun fireing."

The kettledrums appear on the establishment as late as 1756, when Cotterel Barret was kettle-drummer at three shillings per diem, but in 1759 the Artillery was divided into independent brigades or batteries; and as it now ceased to march in one column, as has formerly been the case, the kettle-drums were abolished.[5] The drums and their carriage were deposited in the Tower of London,[6] and in Brayley and Britton's *History of the Tower* are mentioned as being on the ground floor of the

---

[1] *Memoirs of the R.A.*,—MACBEAN.

[2] *British Military Journal*, 1798.

[3] *Artillery Regimental History.*—MILLER.

[4] *England's Artillery.*—BROWNE, 1865.

[5] *Early History of the R.A.*—CLEAVELAND.

[6] At this time there was also a pair of kettledrums preserved in the Tower which, according to Dr. Burney, had been captured at Malplaquet, 1709. These "Tower Drums" were in frequent request by Handel for his Oratorios, and there are documents signed by him acknow-ledging the loan of these drums from the Master-General of Ordnance.

small armoury, but they were probably destroyed in the fire of 1841.

Among other customs brought from Flanders was that of employing fifers as well as drummers:— "The first fifers in the British service," says Colonel Macbean (*Memoirs of the Royal Artillery*, 1743-79), "were established in the Royal Regiment of Artillery at the end of the war, being taught by John Ulrich,[1] a Hanoverian fifer brought from Flanders by Colonel Belford when the Allied Army separated."

A claim of priority in this little particular has been set up for the Guards, by Grose in his *Military Antiquities* (1801), who says that the fife was restored to the army by the Duke of Cumberland, who re-introduced it into the Guards about 1745. There is no mention of the fife, however, in Cumberland's general orders, which are printed in Sime's *Military Guide* (1772), although the drum is frequently mentioned; neither do any fifers appear on the establishment of the Grenadier Guards[2] until 1757, nor in the Coldstream Guards[3] until 1758. There is, however, an interesting engraving by William Hogarth, representing " The March of the Guards towards Scotland in the year 1745," in which a drummer and fifer are depicted. It was painted and published in December, 1750. Grose goes on to say that the fife was not, however, adopted by the marching regiments till the year

[1] He subsequently became fife-major, and was discharged in 1766.

[2] *History of the Grenadier Guards.*—HAMILTON, 1874.

[3] *History of the Coldstream Guards.*—MACKINNON, 1833.

1747 :—" The first regiment that had it was the
19th, then called the Green Howards, in which
I had the honour to serve, and well remember a
Hanoverian youth, an excellent fifer,[1] being given
by his colonel to Lieutenant-Colonel Williams,
then commanding that regiment at Bois-le-Duc,
in Dutch Flanders."

With respect to this assertion, we cannot dis-
credit it; but it is remarkable that Grose makes no
reference to the claim of the Royal Artillery, a
fact that must have been patent to his personal
knowledge. Sir George Grove, in his great work,
A Dictionary of Music and Musicians, gives the
Royal Artillery the credit of the introduction of the
fife. Another work of authority[2] says that it was
introduced at the siege of Maestricht in 1747.
Cannon, in his *Records of the 19th Foot*, shies at the
subject by merely adding a foot-note:—" In the
year 1747, fifes were introduced into the regiments
of infantry."

The historians of the Royal Artillery make no
mention of Grose in this matter, except the author
of *England's Artillerymen*, who maintains that:—
" The use of fifes was revived by the Duke of
Cumberland[3] at the termination of the war in

---

[1] Note that he speaks of a *fifer*, whereas Macbean refers
to *fifers*.

[2] LLOYD'S *Encyclopædic Dictionary*, 1895.

[3] On this point an extract from *Nollekens and his Times*,
by J. I. SMITH (1828), may prove interesting :—" One
morning, when a fifer and drummer were row-de-dowing
to a newly-married couple at the ' Sun and Horseshoe,' at
the opposite house to Nollekens, Mrs. Nollekens observed
that her father, Mr. Welch, used to say that fifing boys
were first introduced by the Duke of Cumberland."

Flanders in 1747, the Royal Artillery being the first regiment to which they were attached. The Guards adopted the use of fifes soon after the Artillery; the first marching regiment to use them was the 19th."

There had been a Drum-Major[1] borne on the establishment of the Cadet Company, R.A., since 1744.[2] The first to hold this office was (I believe) John Hollingshead, who served in that capacity with the regiment in Flanders until 1747, when he was recalled by the following[3] :—

> "WOOLWICH, 16th June, 1747.
>
> " *To* COLONEL BELFORD :
>
> " All our Drummers being at present boys, and three of them lately Enterred,[4] the General desires that you will order the Drum Major to England, as we have nobody here [who] can instruct them to beat."

In the following year (1748) a Fife-Major was added to the regiment. The duties of the Drum-Major and Fife-Major were not only to teach their respective instruments, but it was also part of their

---

[1] Drum-Majors were admitted into our service during the latter part of the reign of Charles I. (Grose). Sir James Turner (*Pallas Armata*, 1683) denies altogether their existence :—" There is," he says, " another inconsiderable staff officer in most armies, yet necessary enough in all regiments of Foot, and that is the Drummer-Major, the French call him Colonel-Drummer. In some places he gets a third more pay than other drummers, but here at home we acknowledge no such creature." Notwithstanding this, the Drum-Major is mentioned by Ward (*Animadversions of Warre*, 1639) and by Venn (*Military and Maritime Discipline*), and his duties defined. I find one on the strength of the Royal Scots in 1639, and in the Coldstream Guards in 1650.

[2] *Records of the R.M. Academy.*—JONES, 1851.

[3] Letter Books, R.A. Record Office.

[4] Enterred—enlisted.

office to inflict corporal punishment upon offenders sentenced to such.[1]

Up to the time of William III. corporal punishments were executed by the Provost-Marshal and his deputies, after that they were carried into effect by the Drum-Major and his drummers.[2]

By this time the Artillery fifers had progressed favourably, and were soon employed to march at the head of the regiment.[3] At a review, held by the King in Green Park on the 13th June, 1753, the Artillery was headed by a Drum-Major, ten drummers, one Fife-Major, and five fifers.

These drum and fife bands were common to all regiments of " Foot,"[4] whilst cavalry regiments had their trumpeter-bands, and these were kept strictly upon the lines of past centuries.

The hautboy was still a favourite with the cavalry and infantry, and it became the nucleus of the military band, as we understand the modern signification of the term. In past years, bands of hautboys played in parts, the bass being given by an instrument called a curtail, an ancient species of bassoon. But since then the hautboy and bassoon had been greatly improved. We are told

---

[1] A curious instruction appears in the *Records of the Coldstream Guards*—MACKINNON (1833) :—" The Drum-Major to be answerable that no cat has more than nine tails."

[2] *History of the British Army.*—SCOTT, 1868.

[3] *England's Artillerymen*—BROWNE, 1865.

[4] It would appear that the fife was used also in the cavalry, for we find that in the Light Dragoons in 1799 the fife was used for playing the quick-march when the troops were dismounted (*Story of the 17th Lancers*—PARRY).

in a military work of 1760 (*Discipline of the Light
Horse*—HINDE) that horns and bassoons were issued
to the trumpeters, which gave them a "band of
musick," consisting of hautbois, trumpets, horns,
bassoons; this was the beginning of the military
band in England.

A new era begins with the introduction and rapid
improvement of the clarionet.[1] Its brilliant tone,
capable of every shade, and its large compass, at
once placed it as the leading instrument, pushing
the hautboy into a second place.

It was in Germany, however, that the modern
military band became properly established. With
them, bands were at first a privilege granted to
but few especially renowned regiments. But it was
found to be such a useful addition, that in time
every regiment obtained one, the members of
which were called "hautboisten" on account of
that instrument being the most prominent. There
was no fixed plan in the instrumentation, the
arrangement of which rested with the Colonel or
Bandmaster.[2]

The military genius and musical instincts of
King Frederick II. (the Great) of Prussia took the
first step in establishing the military band on a
recognised model.[3] This first organisation as fixed
by his order was comprised of two hautboys, two

---

[1] The clarionet is said to have been introduced into
England in 1760 by J. C. Bach, the son of the great
Sebastian Bach.

[2] *Military Music.*—KAPPEY.

[3] *History of Wind Band Music.*—TURPIN.

clarionets, two horns, and two bassoons.[1] This combination, which received the title of " Harmonie Musik," was a great favourite with composers. Beethoven composed an octet in E flat (op. 103) and a rondino in E flat for this combination. Mozart also wrote three serenades for the same.[2]

Frederick the Great's band of eight became generally adopted throughout Europe, for there can be no question that all European nations copied the Germans in matters of military music. Rousseau speaks of the superiority of German military music, and says that the French had few military instruments and few military marches, most of which were *très malfaites*.

Another writer says :—" The English easily adopt innovations from abroad, and complete their military bands easily enough"; which is perhaps true, for one of the earliest, if not *the* earliest, record of a band in our service is one " Made in Germany," and that, the " Band of the Royal Regiment of Artillery," which was formed there in 1762.

---

[1] *Dictionary of Music and Musicians.*—GROVE.

[2] *Verzeichniss Tonwerke Mozarts.*—KÖCHEL, 1862.

From an engraving in the R.A. Institution.

MAJOR-GENERAL W. PHILLIPS, R.A.,

THE FOUNDER

OF THE

ROYAL ARTILLERY BAND.

. . . . and two . . . . . . Th

. . . . the . . of Harmonie

. . . . favourite with composers.

. . . . tet in E flat (op. 103)

. . . . this combination.

. . . . for the same.[2]

. . . . of eight became

. . . . Europe, for there

. . . . . all European nations

. . . . of military music.

. . . the superiority of German

. . . . the French had few

. . . . few military marches,

. . . .

A . . . . . . The English easily

adopt . . . . and complete their

. . . . . band . . . . . . "; which is perhaps

true, for . . . . if not *the* earliest,

record of a . . . . vice is one "Made in

Germany," and that . . . "Band of the Royal

. . . . of Artillery, ... which was formed there

in 176."

[1] *Dictionary of Music and Musicians.* GROVE.

[2] *Verzeichniss sämmtliche Tonwerke Mozarts* — KÖCHEL, 1862.

From an engraving in the R.A. Institution.

MAJOR-GENERAL W. PHILLIPS, R.A.,

THE FOUNDER

OF THE

ROYAL ARTILLERY BAND.

CHAPTER II.

1762-1810.

"I'll no more drumming,
A plague of all drums!"
—"ALL'S WELL THAT ENDS WELL."

" Disputed which the best might be,
For still their music seemed to start
Discordant echoes in each heart."
—LONGFELLOW.

IN August, 1758, a large body of British troops embarked for the Continent to co-operate with the Hanoverians and Hessians in expelling the French from Germany. Captain William Phillips was sent in command of the Royal Artillery attached to the army of H.S.H. Prince Ferdinand of Brunswick. The following year, reinforcements were sent over, and a regular brigade of artillery was established there, consisting of three companies, commanded by Captain Phillips, Captain Macbean, and Captain-Lieutenant Drummond,[1] who at Minden (1759) and Warberg (1760) behaved with great gallantry.

Whilst peace negotiations were in progress (1762), Lieutenant-Colonel Phillips[2] and his officers had excellent opportunities of hearing the very fine

---

[1] This was Captain Cleaveland's company.

[2] He was appointed Brevet-Lieutenant-Colonel in 1760.

bands of their German allies, which were considered the finest in existence.

It must be remembered that the "great kettle-drums" did not accompany the artillery in this campaign, and it is most probable that they were greatly missed, for we find that in 1762, Lieutenant-Colonel Phillips[2] gave instructions for the formation of a band, after the German model, known as the "Royal Artillery Band."[3]

The following are the Articles of Agreement[4] upon which the musicians were engaged. The original is written in both English and German, the last article, in English only, being added by Colonel Phillips himself:—

> i. The band to consist of eight men, who must also be capable to play upon the violoncello, bass, violin and flute, as other common instruments.

---

[1] *Memoirs of the R.A.*—MACBEAN.

[2] William Phillips joined the regiment as a Cadet-Gunner 1746, and appointed Lieutenant-Fireworker 1747, and Second Lieutenant 1755. His later commissions are dated, First Lieutenant, 1st April, 1756; Captain, 12th May, 1756; Brevet-Lieutenant-Colonel, 15th August, 1760; Major, 25th April, 1777; Lieutenant-Colonel, 6th July, 1780. He was appointed Major-General in the Army, August, 1777. He served with great distinction at Minden and Warberg, and later in the American War—at Stillwater and Saratoga. He conducted the retreat from Saratoga in October, 1777, and was second senior officer at the council of war when Burgoyne decided on surrendering to the Republican forces. In 1781 he was sent with 2,000 picked troops to Rhode Island, to prevent the French sailing for the Chesapeake. Here he contracted a disease which, unhappily for his country, was beyond the skill of his physician. He was taken to Petersburg, Virginia, where he died 13th May, 1781.—*Kane's List.*

[3] *England's Artillerymen.*—BROWNE, 1865.

[4] IBID.

ii. The regiment's musick must consist of two trumpets, two French horns, two bassoons, and four hautbois or clarinetts[1]; these instruments to be provided by the regiment, but kept in repair by the head musician.

iii. The musicians will be looked upon as actual soldiers, and cannot leave the regiment without a formal discharge. The same must also behave them, according to the articles of war.

iv. The aforesaid musicians will be clothed by the regiment.

v. So long as the artillery remains in Germany each musician to have ten dollars per month, but the two French horns to have twelve dollars per month, out of which they must provide their own bread; but when they arrive in England, each musician to receive one shilling, the two French horns one shilling and twopence per day; this payment to commence at their arrival in England.

vi. The musicians shall be obliged to wait upon the commanding officer so often as he shall desire to have musick, without any hope of gratification, but if they shall be desired to attend upon any other officer, they are to have a ducat per night, but in England half a guinea.

vii. Should the aforesaid musicians be taken sick they are to be attended by the surgeon of the regiment, for which they are to allow five-pence farthing sterling monthly to be given out of their wages.

viii. The two French horns will enter into pay, as soon as they sign their articles, the pay of the other six musicians, to commence as soon as they arrive at the corps.

ix. [In the handwriting of Colonel Phillips.] Provided the musicians are not found to be good

---

[1] Ten instruments are here provided for eight men.— *Vide* Clause i.

D

performers at their arrival they will be discharged, and at their own expense. This is meant
to make the person who engages the musicians
careful in his choice.

W. PHILLIPS,

Lieut.-Col. Comdt. of British Artillery.[1]

This was the nucleus of a band, a "wind" and
"stringed" band from the first, "which," says
Colonel Duncan, M.P. (*History of the R.A.*) "has
developed into probably the best military band in
the world."

There is, however, no reference to music or
musicians in the muster rolls, nor in the pay
accounts of the companies serving in Germany.
This may easily be accounted for, as the musicians
were not properly attested soldiers, which is very
evident from the Articles of Agreement, which
would have been unnecessary had the musicians
been regularly enlisted.

Peace was proclaimed in November, 1762, and
early in the following year the Artillery commenced
their homeward march through Holland, embarking
at Bremen in June for Woolwich. They had
scarcely got settled in England when these companies were ordered abroad again. Lieutenant-

---

[1] This interesting document was discovered among the
old records of the 1st Battalion R.A. during the "fifties,"
and was claimed for the band by Mr. Smyth, the bandmaster
at that time, into whose custody it was given. After his
death in 1885, enquiries were made by J. A. Browne, Esq.,
the author of *England's Artillerymen*, as to the safety of the
document, when he was informed by Madame Smyth that
she was not aware of its existence. These "Articles of
Agreement" were fortunately copied from the original by
J. A. Browne, Esq., when he was writing *England's
Artillerymen*, and are to be found in the chapter on "Music
in the Royal Artillery."

Colonel Phillips' company was despatched to Minorca, under Captain-Lieutenant Foy, Phillips remaining at Woolwich. The band doubtless remained there also. It was certainly at Woolwich in 1765-8, for the earliest bandmaster of whom there is any record is the one in appointment at this time. It was he who gave the celebrated Irish flautist, Andrew Ashe,[1] his first lessons in music. The latter was born in 1756,[2] and before his ninth year he was sent to an academy near Woolwich, where he remained more than three years.

"At an early age he showed a great disposition for music, and devoted a certain sum of his weekly allowance to the Master of the Artillery Band (who occasionally attended the academy) to receive lessons on the violin."[3]

Although the band was to be considered "the regiment's musick," yet it is far more likely that it was quite a private affair so far as its maintenance was concerned, being supported by the officers of the regiment, perhaps by the 1st Battalion alone, by whom it was raised in Germany. It does not appear to have been officially recognised until the 4th Battalion R.A. was formed in January, 1771, "when the band was taken over and subscribed for by Colonel Ord and the officers of the battalion."[4]

---

[1] For many years principal flute at the Salomon Concerts, where Haydn produced his symphonies; later of the Italian Opera, and for twelve years director of the Bath Concerts.

[2] *Handbook of Musical Biography.*—BAPTIE, 1883.

[3] *A Dictionary of Musicians*, 1824.

[4] *England's Artillerymen.*—BROWNE, 1865.

Colonel Macbean, in his *Memoirs of the Royal Artillery*, says:—"Colonel Ord being appointed Colonel to the new or 4th Battalion, formed a band of eight musicians,[1] which he and the Captains supported till the next year, when this battalion embarked to relieve the 1st Battalion in America, the battalions remaining at home took on themselves to support it."

The musicians were placed on the establishment of the various companies as Matrosses,[2] at ninepence halfpenny per diem. In January, 1773, the Master Musician and the eight private musicians of the Royal Regiment of Artillery are shown upon a separate muster roll and pay list[3]; the former receiving three shillings and sixpence per diem, and the latter one shilling per diem,[4] which together with other items necessary for their maintenance, are charged to the non-effective account of the regiment.

The Band of Musick,
Royal Regiment of Artillery,
January, 1773.

Master Musician - - Antony Rocca.

Private Musicians:

1.	Andrew Peddie.	5. John Bingle.
2.	Stephen Bolitho.	6. Philip Geary.
3.	John Stephens.	7. John Richardson.
4.	John Winslow.	8. William Elliott.

[1] Macbean says it was in 1771 that the band was taken up, but in the *Dickson Memoirs* it appears under the year 1772.

[2] Matrosses—Soldiers in the Artillery next below the gunners. The rank was abolished in 1783, when all private soldiers in the regiment were called gunners.

[3] Muster Rolls, R.A. Record Office.

[4] This was twopence halfpenny more than the private rank (a matross) received, which distinction remains to the present day.

These were placed under the charge of Lieut. Alex. Mackenzie, Quarter-Master in the 3rd Battalion.

Antony Rocca is the first bandmaster whose name I have been able to trace :—

Antony Rocca.

In October, 1771, he is shown as a matross in Lieutenant-Colonel Phillips' Company.[1] He was most probably the leading musician, for in December he is transferred to Anderson's Company as Corporal. Later he appears in Buchanon's Company, and in September, 1772, he is appointed " Master Musision,"[2] a position he held until his death, after a short illness, 16th January, 1774.[3]

The officers now advertised for a master musician, and nine shillings is charged to the non-effective account for the following to be inserted three times in the *Daily Advertiser* :—

" WANTED, immediately, a Person qualified as a Master Musician to a Military Band of Musick,

---

[1] He may have been one of the original band which Lieutenant-Colonel Phillips brought from Germany.

[2] He is also called " Music-Major," " Chief Musician," " Music Master," " Principal Musician," and " Master."

[3] At this period the Royal Artillery had their barracks in the Warren (Royal Arsenal), which were built in 1719. They are now officers' quarters. The present barracks on Woolwich Common were occupied in 1776. This was, however, only the eastern half; the other half was commenced six years later.

who is a perfect Master of the French Horn, and performs on other Wind Instruments, as Great encouragement will be given. None need apply who is not a perfect Master, and can be well recommended as a Person of great Sobriety and good character."

" N.B.—Apply to Mr. George Drummond, at Messrs. Cox and Mair, Craig's Court, Charing Cross, for further particulars."[1]

It is not until May that anyone appears as Master Musician, when Herr Georg Kühler, who afterwards styles himself " George Kealer," is considered a " perfect master," and appointed to lead the band :—

In this year the Master-General and Lieutenant-General of Ordnance were pleased to ease the regiment of that expense[2] incurred by the band, by each contributing one shilling and fourpence farthing per diem towards the expenses of the master musician. The band went to Chatham in this year with the 3rd Battalion, but returned in October.

[1] Muster Rolls, R.A. Record Office.

[2] *Memoirs of the Royal Artillery.*—MACBEAN.

Herr Kühler is succeeded in 1777 by Herr Friedrich Wielle,[1] a very capable musician :—

He was most certainly a much smarter man than either of his predecessors. The increase of his pay to four shillings per diem in 1782, and the frequent, very frequent music bills bear evidence to this. One of these bills is inserted here, as the English of Herr Wielle is very interesting[2] :—

Bought by Fried. Wielle, Music Master, for the use of the Band of Musick belonging to the Royal Regiment of Artillery.

	£	s.	d.
The 5th January, 1787—Due to Mr. Wielle from a Bill from the year 1786		17	9
The 13th February—To a Sett of Frensch Military Concertos		9	0
3 large Drum heads for the Bass Drum		16	0
Caen for Clarinett Rieds		3	6
4 Brass Hucks to the Cimbals		1	6
For two Drum Sticks for ditto			7
The 6th April—For Oil & Caen for the Clarinetts ...		5	0
10 Bassoon Rieds at 1 Shill. each		10	0
2 Large Drum heads for the Tamborins		6	6
The 5th June—To a Leder skin for the use of the Bass Drum		3	0
For making it into a Breeches[3]		1	9
The 1st August—For 6 Bassoon Rieds at 1 Shill. each		6	0
The 4th November—For a Drum Card		1	5
For Oil & Caen for the instruments		4	6
The 11th April, 1788—For Oil & Caen for the instruments		8	6
12 Bassoon Rieds at 1 Shill. each		12	0
For 2 Setts of Millitary Concertos	1	1	0
Music Paper		16	0
	£7	5	7

[1] The author of *England's Artillerymen* mentions (on the authority of Mr. McKenzie, who served in the band from 1795-1845) a Mr. Bennett, who was bandmaster before Herr Wielle, but I can find no trace of him on the muster rolls or pay lists at the Record Office.

[2] Muster Rolls, R.A. Record Office.

[3] He evidently means an apron, not " a breeches."

The band was ordered on duty to Coxheath Camp, near Colchester, in 1778, and again in 1803. On the latter occasion it was presented with a handsome side drum by the Master-General of Ordnance, inscribed :—

PRESENTED TO THE ROYAL ARTILLERY BAND
AT
COXHEATH CAMP
BY THE
EARL OF CHATHAM,
MASTER-GENERAL OF THE ORDNANCE,
1803.

This was most probably the first side drum used by the band. For many years this old instrument was lost sight of, until 1881, when Captain Morgan, the Band Secretary, informed the Band Committee[1] that this drum was in the possession of a local instrument maker, who did odd repairing work for the band, from whom it was gleaned that the drum was originally a long drum of the Guards' pattern, and was given to him to cut down, to furnish two smaller ones.

The drum was purchased back by the officers for three pounds, and handed over to the care of the band, but in 1894 it was considered advisable to deposit it in the R.A. Institution, where it remains at present.

During the whole five years that Rocca and Kühler were "masters," there had been only one alteration in the *personnel* of the band; but from the many changes during the early years of Herr Wielle's *régime*, it would appear that the talents of

[1] *R.A. Band Committee Proceedings, &c.,* 1881.

the musicians were not to his satisfaction. He
begins with discharging two of them within a year,
and in less than six years eighteen musicians are
tried in the ranks of the "band of musick."[1]

The muster roll in January, 1784, was :—

Master Musician	-	-	Friedrich Wielle.

Private Musicians :

1.	Carly Franky.	5.	Anton Reichenbach.
2.	Joseph Hampton.	6.	Frantz Sternberg.
3.	Carl Daumichen.	7.	Georg Spindler.
4.	Andreas John.	8.	John Schroeder.

From this we see that the whole of the band, with
one exception, were foreigners; in fact, it became
to be generally understood in England that no
one but a foreigner knew anything of musical
matters. At one time the rage was for Italians, at
another for Germans, and the result was that
though a few very excellent musicians were thus
imported, the majority were needy adventurers,
and the result disastrous for military music in
England.

Whether this importation of foreign bandsmen
into the Royal Artillery was a fad of the officers,
or the extreme partiality of Herr Wielle for his
own countrymen, cannot be said; but one thing is
certain : these musicians did not come within the
expectations of their masters, for they are very
soon superseded by native talent, and in November,

---

[1] By this means he gets rid of all the old members of
the band. The last of the old band to leave was Andrew
Peddie, who was pensioned with sixpence per diem. After
a little time, this musician presents a memorial to the
Board of Ordnance, begging for an increase in his pension
to ninepence, on account of his " disorder," which incapa-
citated him from further employment.

1787, six out of the eight musicians are English. The list of the band is given here, as this is the last time that they appear on one muster-roll[1]:—

Master Musician - -	Friedrich Wielle.

Private Musicians :

1. Joseph Hampton.	5. John Carson.
2. Anton Reichenbach.	6. John A. Vernan.
3. John Schroeder.	7. Jacob Henry.
4. James Emerson.	8. James Lambert.

There is an interesting letter[2] which might serve to show that even at this period the bandsmen of the Royal Artillery were musicians of talent, and that their services were in demand outside their military capacity:—

"CHATHAM BARRACKS,
"27th January, 1787.
"COLONEL MACBEAN,
"SIR,—I shall esteem it a favour if you will permit Charles Dimechin of your band to come here for two or three days.[3]
"I am, Sir, etc.,
"EDMD. EYRE, Lt.-Col., 64th Regt."

In November, 1787, some question arises at the Ordnance Office concerning the maintenance of the band, and the paymaster requests that Major Macleod, the Brigade Major at Woolwich, "will

---

[1] Muster Rolls, R.A. Record Office.

[2] Letter Books, R.A. Record Office.

[3] The letter says nothing why the Colonel of the 64th Regiment should want a musician of the R.A. for "two or three days." It may have been an ordinary engagement, but more likely than not he was engaged to train a band for this regiment; as it was about this period that the line regiments began to raise bands. He takes his discharge, moreover, a few months later.

have the goodness to inform him by what Authority or Order the Extra expence of the Master of the Band is charged to the Master-General and Lieut.-General of the Ordnance each Half. The Surveyor-General of the Ordnance allowing only 9½d., the pay of a Mattross per Diem, with the addition of sixpence granted by the Board to be charged to the Non-effective Acct. of the Regt."[1]

Major Macleod's answer to the Board cannot be found, but he must have given a sufficient explanation, for the charge against the Master and Lieut.-General remains unchanged. It, however, opened the eyes of the Board to the necessity of placing the musicians upon the establishment of the regiment, and so reduce the enormous drain on the non-effective accounts, by which the band was kept up. The pay alone of the master and eight musicians amounted to two hundred and nineteen pounds per annum; so the Board now decided to place the eight musicians upon the strength of the various companies, to be paid as musicians at one shilling per diem, thus reducing the charge on the non-effective accounts by one hundred and forty-six pounds per annum. The "master musician" still continued to be paid from the old source, but his daily pay was reduced three shillings.[2]

In 1772 and 1775, the Royal Artillery was reviewed by King George III. on both occasions at Blackheath.[3] His Majesty visited Woolwich in

---

[1] Letter Books, R.A. Record Office.
[2] Muster Rolls, R.A. Record Office.
[3] *History of the R.A.*—DUNCAN, 1872.

state in 1773, and was received on the parade by Lord Townshend, the Master-General of Ordnance, and after the salute had been fired, "the drums and music beat the march."[1]   Again, on the 9th July, 1788, George III. reviewed the R.A., and was on the Barrack Field at the early hour of 6.20 a.m. On this occasion the regiment was formed up in two ranks, quite an innovation, and the king having ridden down them, the regiment formed in open column, and marched past in slow and quick time. The band was specially augmented for this great occasion by two private instrumentalists :—" Adam Lessler and Raie Jones, engaged by order of the Master-General to play with the band of musick the seventh and ninth of July at one guinea each day, and half-a-crown for lodging, etc., the nights preceding."[2]

Although at this time there were several bands in the service, yet the instrumentation was of the most meagre description.   The three regiments of foot guards had bands; and these most probably rank next to the Royal Artillery as the oldest bands in the service.   Parke, in his *Musical Memoirs*, tells us that the bands of the three regiments of foot guards consisted in 1783 of only eight performers, viz. :—two hautboys, two clarionets, two horns. and two bassoons.   They were civilians, excellent performers, who were hired by the month; their only military duty being to play the King's Guard

---

[1] *Records of Woolwich.*—VINCENT.

[2] Muster Rolls, R.A. Record Office.

from the parade at Horse Guards to St. James's Palace and back. On one occasion the colonel of the Coldstream Guards desired his band to play during an aquatic excursion to Greenwich, and ordered them to attend. This the musicians declined to do, as such work was beyond the scope of their engagement. The officers, who alone supported the band, being desirous of having a band which they could command on all occasions, wrote to the Duke of York, the colonel of the regiment, who was at that time in Hanover, stating their wishes, to which His Royal Highness assented. In 1785, according to the regimental records, a band of regularly attested soldiers were enlisted in Hanover by the Duke and sent to England. It consisted of twelve performers, four clarionets, two bassoons, two hautboys, two French horns, one trumpet, and one serpent.

The band of the Honourable Artillery Company in 1783 was comprised of four clarionets, two horns, two bassoons and one trumpet.[1] Eight to twelve musicians were still the recognised number for military bands.[2] However, in the process of time new instruments were introduced, which necessitated an increase in numbers. The first instruments to be added to the time-honoured "Harmonie Musik" combination were instruments of percussion. This new departure also emanated

---

[1] *History of the Honourable Artillery Company.*—RAIKES.

[2] As late as 1820, the Minister of War in France considered eight musicians sufficient for a military band.

from Germany, and from Frederick the Great.[1] We find them later in Austria,[2] but it is not until about 1785-7 that percussion instruments are found in our military bands, and their introduction is credited to the Duke of York,[3] who brought or sent percussion instrumentalists over from Germany for the band of the Coldstream Guards.[4] From this date military music " grew burning bright with fife-shriek, cymbal crash, and trumpet blast " (Browning).

It then became " good style " to employ black men to play these instruments.[5] These men were dressed in the most extravagant Eastern style, with gorgeous slashed tunics, loose jackets, and high feathered turbans, and in addition to playing the bass drum, side drum, cymbals, and triangle, an

---

[1] In the early years of the eighteenth century, when the fame of the Janissary bands was at its height, Frederick the Great obtained one from the Sultan. They usually consisted of a few, about six *sarzas* (hautboys) and fifes, and about a dozen drums, cymbals and triangles. So pleased was he with the imposing appearance of these oriental musicians, that he introduced percussion instruments into all his military bands (*Military Music*—KAPPEY).

[2] Frederick Nicolai, who visited Vienna in 1781, speaks in high praise of a military band which was comprised of two *shawns* (? hautboys), two clarionets, two horns, one trumpet, two bassoons, and a side and bass drum.

[3] *Court and Private Life in the time of Queen Charlotte.* —PAPENDIEK, 1887.

[4] *Musical Memoirs.*—PARKE.

[5] They had been, however, employed as trumpeters and drummers quite forty years before this. The Royal Horse Guards had black trumpeters in 1742, and the 29th Foot had black drummers in 1759.

instrument, known as the "Jingling Johnnie,"[1] and tambourines were employed. In a letter of W. J. Mattham, innkeeper at Lavenham,[2] we are given the composition of the band of the West Middlesex Militia at this date, which he says "had the best band I ever heard, 'tis worth mentioning to those who are lovers of superior music. It consisted of five clarionets, two French horns, one bugle-horn, one trumpet, two bassoons, one bass drum, two triangles (the latter played by boys about nine years old), two tambourines (the performers mullatoes), and the clash pans by a real blackamoor, a very active man[3] who walked between the two mullatoes, which had a very grand appearance indeed." The black men were employed in the Foot Guards until as late as the Crimean War, but they were dispensed with in most bands before 1837.

Percussion instruments were in use by the R.A. Band in 1787, for cymbals, tambourines, and a bass

---

[1] This was a pole surmounted by a crescent, from which depended bells. In the Janissary days it was the standard of the band, and had a number of dyed horse tails hanging to it, but no bells. It was called by them "Mahomet's Standard," and by the European nations, with whom it lost its ancient dignity by the addition of bells, it was called "Chapeau Chinois," and in England "Jingling Johnnie." The instrument is depicted in an old sketch, by Cruikshank, of a foot regiment marchiug to church. It has been superseded some years now by an instrument called the glockenspiel.

[2] *History of the British Army.*—SCOTT, 1868.

[3] This "very active man" that played the "clash-pans" (cymbals) was evidently one of those men who could, as the Irish expressively term it, "cut a caper." An old Woolwich resident once assured the writer that his grandfather well remembered the "blacks" of the R.A. Band, marching in front, performing all sorts of contortions and evolutions whilst playing their tambourines.

drum are mentioned in the music bill previously quoted.[1] Three black men were employed to play these instruments, who are shown on the establishment in 1812.

But matters were overdone in this particular, and some bands actually had one-third of its members performing upon percussion instruments. They had the good sense, however, to introduce more wind instruments to reduce this preponderance of noise. Perhaps the first to be taken up was the serpent, a large wooden instrument covered with leather, curved in shape (hence the name), and played with a metal- or bone-cupped mouthpiece.[2] The flute and trombone followed soon afterwards.

These additions seem to have taken root very early in the R.A. Band, for we find that in 1789 the musicians are increased from eight to nine. In 1792, when it is ordered on duty to Bagshot, we find that there are ten musicians, and in a few months eleven musicians are granted.[3]

However, in 1794 the band numbers ten musicians and a master musician, besides supernumeraries who were admitted into its ranks during the year.[4] Again, in 1802, the band is further augmented to twenty-one.[5] This was due to the incorporation of

[1] According to J. A. Kappey (GROVE's *Dictionary of Music*,—Art.: Wind Band), these instruments were not introduced into military bands until 1805-8 (?).

[2] It was superseded quite fifty years ago by the bombardon.

[3] Letter Books, R.A. Record Office.

[4] *England's Artillerymen.*—BROWNE, 1865.

[5] *History of the R.A.*—DUNCAN, 1872.

the Royal Irish Artillery with the Royal Artillery in 1801. The band of the former, numbering about thirty-five, were sent to Woolwich, and the best musicians were absorbed into the R.A. Band, those least proficient, including three or four of the old band, being discharged.

The band now consisted of :—

```
 1 Master
 1 Sergeant
 2 Corporals
18 Musicians ¹
 —
22
```

At this period, bands were dressed and equipped according to the tastes and financial resources of the officers, but it is difficult to realise in these days the eccentric fashion, sometimes bordering on the grotesque, in which some bands were presented to the public gaze. The most general practice was to dress the band in the colour of the regiment's facings,² and as these were at that time very varied in hue, bands were to be seen in coats of red, blue, black, buff, white, orange, yellow, and green; the

---

¹ This rank—Musician—still continues, and is peculiar only to the Royal Artillery. In all other corps the members of the band are privates, etc., and for distinction sake called "bandsmen."

² It has been the custom for centuries to dress military musicians differently, and in a more superior way to the rank and file. In the accounts of the Norwich contingent, 1587-8, there is a charge for coats, which were of "bayes and carseys" (kersey), "and whight yncle to laye upon the same." The drummer's coat was of "grene carsey," embellished with eleven yards of lace and six yards of pointing. In the contract for the clothing of an infantry regiment in 1693, the men wore grey coats and breeches, and the drummer a purple coat and grey breeches.

latter in seven different shades. A recent writer
in the *Woolwich Herald* says that the R.A. Band at
this period "were clothed in scarlet coatees with
blue facings, just the opposite to the dress of the
men, cocked hats, white knee breeches and black
gaiters."[1]

This must have been their "dress suit," for we
are informed that they wore "plain coats,"[2] which
were probably the same as those of the regiment.
At this period both officers and men wore their hair
"clubbed," *i.e.*, plaited and turned up, being tied
with black ribbon or tape. Those whose hair,
being so short, could not be plaited, were provided
with false plaits. Among the "necessaries" of an
artillery soldier at this time was a powder bag and
puff, four white shirts, six false collars, and a white
stock.[3] The custom of wearing the hair in plaits
or queues was not abolished until 1805, when the
hair was ordered to be worn short.

In 1789 the Brigade-Major asks the Secretary of
the Board of Ordnance to supply the band with
"ten shoulder belts such as are delivered to the
Regiment of Artillery. I venture to make this
demand," he says, "for the musicians having no
sword belts, and having never yet been supplied,
require something of the kind to appear uniform."[4]

On the 1st October, 1798, the Commandant

---

[1] This was no doubt in accordance with the clothing
regulations of July 1st, 1751.

[2] Letter Books, R.A. Record Office.

[3] *History of the Dress of the R.A.*—MACDONALD.

[4] Letter Books, R.A. Record Office.

requests the Honourable Board for some improvement in their uniform :—

> "The band have been hitherto clothed in common without any ornaments whatever, but they have a dress suit which costs a considerable sum, and which has not been asked for these twelve or fourteen years, because the change of the men and the men's natural growth, the cloaths would not fit them after the second year.
>
> "Instead of this I would request the Honourable Board would permit me annually to lay out in ornaments upon the clothing about thirty shillings for each of the twelve men doing duty as musicians, and upon each of their hats a sum not exceeding five shillings.
>
> "I have the honour, etc.,
>
> "V. LLOYD, M.-General."[1]

Herr Wielle, who for twenty-five years had been Master of the Band, took his discharge, with a pension of three shillings and sixpence per diem (1802). He became bandmaster of a dragoon regiment, and later the Sussex Militia. He resided for many years in Mill Lane, Woolwich, subsequently retiring to Hanover, his native place.

Another German was appointed to the position— Herr G. Schnuphass, "a gentleman not distinguished for his musical abilities."[2]

---

[1] Letter Books, R.A. Record Office.
[2] *England's Artillerymen.*—BROWNE, 1865.

He died in 1805, when Herr M. Eishenherdt received the appointment. About this time the band was placed under the sole command of Colonel Charles A. Quist, the Commanding Officer of the Riding Establishment, whose portrait hangs in the R.A. Institution; "and to him was due in a great measure the excellence to which the band attained in the early years of the past century."[1]

When we look at the mechanism of the wood-wind instruments of this time in our museums, and consider the imperfect scale of the brass family, we can quite understand the acclamation with which the introduction of a complete family of keyed brass instruments was received. The first really successful instrument of this type was the key-bugle, called the "Kent-bugle," out of compliment to the Duke of Kent,[2] who as Commander-in-Chief, encouraged its introduction, and soon became the mainstay of our bands. Although it was patented by Halliday, the bandmaster of the Cavan Militia, as his own invention, yet it was simply an improvement of an idea known half a century before.[3] It was made in several sizes, the bass form having the name of ophicleide.

Ancient military music was written, especially for the brass, in the key of C, and even in the first part of the nineteenth century there was still a feeling in favour of the employment of clarionets, bugles, trumpets and horns in C. The score of

[1] *England's Artillerymen.*—BROWNE, 1865.
[2] *Dictionary of Music, &c.*—GROVE.
[3] *Military Music.*—KAPPEY.

Mendelssohn's[1] overture in C (op. 24), written about 1824 for a wind band, has parts for F and C clarionets, basset horns in F, trumpets and horns in C. A good illustration of an arrangement for a military band a century ago is in the "March of the Scottish Archers," which is written for two hautboys, two clarionets in D, two trumpets in D, two horns in D, and a bassoon[2]; and also in a musical supplement presented with the *British Military Journal* of 1799, which is a march, very simple, written for two horns in B, two clarionets, and fagotti.

Of the exact composition of the R.A. Band at this period we have no knowledge,[3] but there is a notice of its performance on the occasion of the Jubilee festivities at Woolwich in 1811, when we are told that "Handel's 'Coronation Anthem' was played by the band of the Royal Artillery with fine effect."[4] This was, however, under a new bandmaster, an Englishman, named George McKenzie, who had risen to the position from the ranks of the band. He succeeded Herr Eishenherdt in 1810, who having married a lady with a fortune, retired from the service to Greenwich, where he died.[5]

[1] Cherubini, Spontini, Berlioz, Kühner, and Meyerbeer have also written for the military (wind) band.

[2] *Musical Educator.* —GREIG.

[3] GROSE (*Military Antiquities*, 1801) gives us an idea of a band at this period. He says :—"Of late years each regiment of infantry has its band of music. The instruments are chiefly hautbois, clarinets, French horns, bassoons, trumpets, cymbals, and in some the tabor [side drum] and pipe [? fife or flute]."

[4] *Records of Woolwich.*—VINCENT, 1890.

[5] *England's Artillerymen.*—BROWNE, 1865.

From a photo.

G. M Kinree

CHAPTER III.

1870-1855.

"He falls with his power all t... ...
Was aught ever heard like his ...

GEORGE McKENZIE ... ...
Brooklyn, Long ... ...
and was the son ... ...
officer in the Royal Art... ...
war of the American Revolut... ...
the battle of Guilford.

The recital of an ... ...
after his birth may prove ... ...

One very cold night in ... ...
about ten o'clock, Mrs. M'K... ...
her infant on her knee ... ...
a tremendous rap on the ... ...
fellows, apparently sail... ...
shut the door ... kly after ... ...
immediately, and laying a ... ... on the
table containing ... thing ... heavy,
ash... some ... dy It ... ped, and
payin... ly for it, proceed ... enjoy it,
making ... ant allusions ... to one ... to the
... handker ... ... ghed heartily
anwhile.

... and's 1855

G. McKenzie

CHAPTER III.

1810-1845.

" He fills with his power all their hearts to the brim,
Was aught ever heard like his fiddle and him ? "
—WORDSWORTH.

GEORGE McKENZIE was born at Fort Brooklyn, Long Island, America, in 1780, and was the son of a non-commissioned officer in the Royal Artillery, who served in the war of the American Revolution, and wounded at the battle of Guilford.

The recital of an incident which occurred shortly after his birth may prove interesting.[1]

One very cold night in the winter of 1780-1, about ten o'clock, Mrs. McKenzie was sitting with her infant on her knee, when she was startled by a tremendous rap on the door, and three young fellows, apparently sailors, entered the hut and shut the door quickly after them. They laughed immoderately, and, laying a handkerchief on the table containing something evidently very heavy, asked for some brandy. It was supplied, and paying handsomely for it, proceeded to enjoy it, making frequent allusions, one to the other, to the contents of the handkerchief, and laughed heartily meanwhile.

[1] *England's Artillery.*—BROWNE, 1865.

On leaving they very warmly thanked Mrs. McKenzie for the shelter she had afforded them, saying she had rendered them a very great service. One of them, stepping back to her, said :—" If you should ever want anything done for this child, ask for the officer who is now the senior midshipman of the ' Prince George.' "

Next morning New York was in alarm, and a large reward was offered for the person or persons who had knocked the head off the statue of William Pitt and carried it away.

Prince William, Duke of Clarence, was at this time serving as midshipman on board Admiral Digby's ship, the " Prince George," though no enquiries were ever made as to whether His Royal Highness was one who had taken shelter in the artilleryman's hut at Port Brooklyn.

Fifty-five years afterwards, when the King, William IV., was speaking to Mr. McKenzie, he asked him of his birth and parentage, and doubtless His Majesty thought of the Pitt's head adventure when he received the bandmaster's answer.

George McKenzie joined "the regiment" as a fifer when only twelve years old (1792), and the following year was sent to Brecknock, Wales, on recruiting service. Here he was taken notice of by the organist of the parish church, St. David's, who being greatly interested in the boy, gave him gratuitous lessons in music.

In 1795 he joined the Royal Artillery Band as a supernumerary, and worked his way first to musician (1798), then to corporal (1806), and on the 5th May,

1810, at the recommendation of Colonel Quist, he was appointed " Master of the Band." He devoted a deal of attention to the string band, which he brought to a high state of efficiency, and he may fairly be claimed as the father of the string band, since it was under his tutelage that it began to assume that position which it has proudly held for so many years.

At the suggestion of the Band Commandant, Colonel Quist, a series of vocal and orchestral concerts, known as the " Royal Artillery Concerts," were instituted about 1810-15. These were held weekly during the winter months at the R.A. Officers' Mess.[1] The services of some of the most distinguished musicians in London were obtained to lead the band,[2] who, with the assistance of some of the officers who were able to play, were enabled to get up concerts of the highest order. The chamber music, &c., of Boccherini, Corelli, Felton and other of the old masters[3] whose compositions were

[1] These concerts, which have continued until the present day, are not to be confounded with those held in the Officers' Mess at present (usually on Thursdays—" Guest Night "). The former are perhaps the oldest concerts in the kingdom, having been inaugurated contemporary with those of the Philharmonic Society.

[2] Conductors as we know them at present were practically unknown at this period. Orchestras were directed by the leader; and it is not until 1820 that the conductor wields his bâton in front of the orchestra, which change is due to Spohr, who, it is said, insisted on conducting in this manner at the Philharmonic Concerts.

[3] The identical parts of the chamber music played at these early concerts are in the writer's possession. They bear the autographs of George McKenzie, the bandmaster, and Captain Percy Drummond, an officer who frequently played the 'cello with the band, and afterwards became the band commandant.

fashionable at that time, and occasionally a symphony of Haydn's, Pleyel's, or Mozart's, in addition
to the light music which had hitherto been the
principal feature of the orchestral performances,
was the music performed at these concerts.

In later years, when the symphonies of Beethoven
and the overtures of Rossini became known, they were
purchased for the band by a Mr. Elliot, an amateur
who took a great interest in its performances.

Among the professionals engaged to lead the
band at these concerts may be mentioned—Nicolas
Mori and Spagnoletti, the eminent violinists, who
where leaders and directors of the Philharmonic
Concerts. Robert Lindley, the celebrated English
'cellist, and Louis Drouet, the divine flute player,
were also engaged on these occasions. Another distinguished musician was Sir Benjamin Bloomfield,
afterwards Lord Bloomfield, who frequently played
'cello solos, and occasionally took part in a duet
with Lindley, his performance being only second to
that eminent instrumentalist. This officer owed
his introduction to court to his musical talents.

His Lordship was greatly interested in the performances of the band, and used every effort to
improve it. On one occasion, when it was playing
in the Arsenal, Lord Bloomfield was so displeased
at the inattention paid to the " piano " passages that
he came out of his quarters in a rage, and assuming
the office of conductor, made the performers repeat
the piece they were playing with such attention
to the marks that the effect was electrical.[1]

---

[1] *England's Artillerymen*—BROWNE, 1865.

The professionals who played at these early concerts occasionally recommended members of the band to play amongst the nobility. On one occasion Mr. McKenzie and three of the band, with the celebrated 'cellist, James Cervetto, gave a concert of chamber music before Queen Caroline and her friends.[1]

Mr. McKenzie conducted several local harmonic societies and glee clubs; and the thought occurred to him that a vocal association might be formed in connection with the band. He accordingly conferred with two of the band, who came from the Duke of Richmond's Band, and possessed excellent voices, Morris (tenor) and Downham (bass).

The first performance of a glee at the concerts so delighted the officers that it was determined to promote the cultivation of a full choir, and an order was instantly given for the enlistment of four boys to sing the treble parts.

Shortly after the singing class was formed, a concert was given in honour of the visit of the Prince Regent, by Sir William Congreve, at his house in Charlton. The Prince having been informed by Colonel Bloomfield that some of the band were good singers, requested them to sing "The Ram of Derby," and added that he would assist. Corporal Morris sang first tenor, and Mr. McKenzie second tenor, His Royal Highness taking the bass part. The band were not only delighted with the honour of singing with the Prince, but charmed beyond measure with his

[1] *England's Artillerymen.*—BROWNE. 1865.

voice, and the artistic manner in which he executed his part.[1]

There is an anecdote related of His Majesty. It was while he was Prince Regent, and during a grand review at Woolwich he espied the "big drummer" of the band, a very aged man, who "hailed" from Wiltshire. The Prince rode up to him, speaking to him kindly, saying that he had remarked to the Commandant that he (the drummer) being such "a very old man," he would be pleased to do something for him. Just before he rode off he told the drummer that he would speak to his father, the King, concerning him, who would probably allow him to be admitted into Chelsea Hospital. This was too much for the aged rhythmic musician, who had, ever since the Prince first addressed him, been building "castles in the air," and no sooner had His Royal Highness mentioned Chelsea Hospital than the old man suddenly retorted : "Well, you tell him I 'on't go !"

The establishment of the R.A. Band in 1812 was :—[2]

> 1 Master
> 1 Sergeant
> 2 Corporals
> 18 Musicians
> 13 Bandamen (drummers and boys)
> 3 Blacks[3]
> ──
> 38

---

[1] *England's Artillerymen.*—BROWNE, 1865.

[2] From a document in the possession of J. A. Browne, Esq.

[3] These played the bass drum, cymbals, and "Jingling Johnnie."

In December, 1820, permission was granted for the R.A. Band to play at the Officers' Mess once a week, generally on a Thursday (guest night), but was not to be detained after 10 p.m.[1] A small sum of money was allowed to the band for this duty, which in the early days was distributed among the principal instrumentalists.

Colonel Quist, the Band Commandant, died on the 26th November, 1821, having reached the great age of ninety-one, and was buried at Plumstead Churchyard. His death was sorely felt by the band. He loved music, and was like a father to all those under his command. He covered their faults, extolled their virtues, and did all in his power to make them comfortable, frequently paying them from his own purse when they were engaged any extra time at a mess concert, etc.[2]

The command of the band was now given to Colonel Percy Drummond, a tolerable musician who had been taught the 'cello by Ashley. He was also very kind to the band, and took every opportunity of promoting its interest.[3]

The band was in frequent attendance at Kensington Palace at this time, the Duchess of Kent (Queen Victoria's mother) and the Duke of Sussex taking a great interest in its performances. The former brought a quantity of music from Germany purposely for the band. We also find them playing at aristocratic parties at Fulham and Thames

[1] *R.A. Mess at Woolwich.*—ROBERTSON.
[2] *England's Artillerymen.*—BROWNE, 1865.
[3] Some music still in use by the band bears his autograph, notably the " Clock Symphony."

Ditton; also at the shows of the Horticultural Society at Chiswick.

At this time all the regiments of guards and many[1] regiments of cavalry and infantry had raised bands, but it is said that the best military bands at the beginning of the nineteenth century were those attached to the militia.[2] This is easily accounted for. First, the musicians were engaged, not enlisted as soldiers, and probably refused to go abroad. Secondly, the colonels and officers of the militia were generally wealthy noblemen and gentlemen resident in the counties, and well able to maintain these bands. Moreover, the regiments of the line had been too seriously engaged in war to pay much attention to bands.

Most regiments in the Peninsular had their bands with them, and we read of their gallantry at Busaco, Talavera, etc. An interesting account of the band of the 48th Foot during this campaign is to be found in *Mary Ann Wellington*[3] by the Rev. R. Cobbold. It is feared, however, that these bands earned an experience somewhat similar to that afterwards obtained at the Crimea. An old Peninsular officer said[4] that he never felt so

---

[1] It is evident that not all regiments had them, from the fact that the 4th Light Dragoons did not commence to form a military band until 1832 (*Music and Musicians*—MARR, 1887).

[2] Mr. Charles Godfrey, founder of the famous Godfrey family, and for forty years bandmaster of the Coldstream Guards, was originally a bassoon player in the Surrey Militia. John Distin, the famous trumpeter and founder of the Distin family, came from the South Devon Militia.

[3] She was the daughter of a gunner in the R.A. who was killed at Cadiz.

[4] *British Bandsman*, April, 1888.

ashamed of our meanness and neglect of military prestige, as when he marched into Paris in 1814, and heard the fine bands of other nationalities, comparing them to the meagre and scanty musical display of the British troops present.[1]

During the forty years' peace which followed the treaty of Paris, the British Army had ample leisure in which to develop its taste for military bands, and a great many changes took place in military music, which entirely altered its character, and removed the limitations of wind bands generally. The first was the invention of the valve, and its application to nearly all brass instruments. It was was first brought out successfully by John Shaw, who designed the upright "clear bore" valve, which he applied to the trumpet in 1824.[2] Some years later it was placed on the market by Embach, of Amsterdam, in instruments called cornopeans (now known as cornets), which were introduced into our bands by John Köhler. This instrument entirely superseded the key-bugle, but for many

---

[1] At the grand ball, given by the Duke of Wellington at Paris, on the occasion of the Order of the Bath being bestowed on Blücher and others, a traveller notes that a military band played in the court of the hotel, but he does not say anything about its playing, or even mentions its name, while in a subsequent chapter he states with what pleasure he listened to the celebrated band of the Emperor of Austria, whose performance "surpassed that of any military orchestra I ever heard." (*Journal of a Tour to Waterloo and Paris in company with Sir Walter Scott in 1815*, by JOHN SCOTT.)

[2] The idea of the valve, although not as we understand it at present, has really to be credited to Claggett, of Dublin, who applied it to the horn about 1775. Blühmel first conceived the proper idea of the valve about 1813, which was brought out by Stölzel as his own invention.

years, indeed, until Kœnig made known its true
character and capabilities, it was chiefly employed
as an accompanying instrument, in fact, as an
assistant to the trumpet.

Bands of music were considered by the War
Office, so purely a matter of luxury that it only
allowed one private in each troop or company to
be trained as a musician, and a sergeant to act as
master of the band. So strict were the authorities
in this particular, that General Officers of districts
were required to report half-yearly that bands under
their command were kept within the regulation
limit, and that they could " play in correct time,"[1]
etc.

All the extra expense for a professional teacher
or bandmaster, and the cost of instruments and
music, was borne by the officers,[2] who subscribed
towards a band fund.

As a matter of course, a certain rivalry soon
arose between the different regiments as to the
superiority of their bands. Wealthy corps would
engage highly trained professional men, mostly from
the continent, at high salaries, and obtain the best
instruments procurable.

Each band was formed on its own model, using
instruments of whatever kind or pitch the colonel
or bandmaster liked. We therefore meet with
some very curious combinations. The Elthorne
Middlesex Militia had a band of " pandean reeds,"
for which the bandmaster, H. Eberhardt, published

---

[1] *General Regulations for the Army*, 1811.
[2] *Military Music.*—KAPPEY.

a tutor. The preface states that :—" The Pandean Reeds are instruments now used in regimental bands, and much approved in the King's Guards." In another part he says :—" The B fifes or flutes serve as an excellent support to the reeds." And further on the reader is told to observe that :— " Where an accidental note occurs, as G sharp or C natural, it must be taken by the flutes or fifes."

The *United Service Journal* for June, 1831, gives us an idea of the mounted band of the 2nd Life Guards at this date, for we are told that :—" After saluting and marching past the King . . . . ' God save the King ' was played by the famous Russian chromatic trumpet band of the regiment (the only one in England)."

Although these bands were allowed, yet there was only one band in the service that was officially recognised and provided for in the Army Estimates.[1] This was the Royal Artillery Band, and payments were granted for one master,[2] one sergeant, two corporals, and eighteen musicians ; and, in addition, £100 was allowed annually for the supply of music and instruments.

It was the custom at this period to dress military bandsmen in white, and it is almost certan that the white uniform worn by the R.A. Band at this date (1830) was introduced by Colonel Quist about 1806.[3]

---

[1] Army Estimates (Office of Ordnance), 1832. The only other grant for music was for a " Sergeant acting as Master of the Band " of the Royal Military College, Sandhurst, at three shillings per diem. (Army Estimates, 1833-4.)

[2] The Bandmaster of the R.A. is shown on the Army Estimates as early as 1823.

[3] *R.A. Institution Proceedings*, Vol. xiv.

F

This white dress became so popular that after William IV. came to the throne it was adopted by all infantry bands. Much licence was allowed in matters of detail, and hence we find many of the band coatees lavishly braided, while brass scales, wings and epaulettes adorned the shoulders. Many line bands wore a bearskin busby, but the majority had the shako. The uniform of the R.A. Band was perhaps the most gorgeous in the service.

The coatee was of fine white cloth with blue facings, edged with silk braid of red, yellow and blue. The front was trimmed with two rows of silk bows of red, yellow and blue, from the centre of which depended silk tassels of the same colours. The epaulettes were of fine wire, covered with yellow twill silk. The trousers were of light blue, tight fitting, with three-quarter-inch stripes of red, yellow and blue silk.[1] The head-dress was a tall shako of black felt, with patent leather peak; the brass plate in front (bearing the Ordnance arms) was surmounted by a scarlet hackle feather plume, thirteen inches high; brass scales at the sides, and hat lines of black mohair.[2]

The bandmaster wore a similar uniform, except that the lacing on the coatee was of gold, in the place of yellow silk, and his epaulettes were of gold. His trousers had, in addition, two huge Austrian knots of gold in front. The bandmaster and band sergeant wore a scarlet waist sash.

[1] White trousers were worn during the summer months.
[2] A winter head-dress was also worn. It was a "frame hat" of whalebone, covered with oilskin, without any ornament except the hat lines.

MUSICIAN,
ROYAL ARTILLERY BAND,
1830.

MUSICIAN,

ROYAL ARTILLERY BAND,

1830.

The leathern stock, common throughout the army, was not worn by the band; a stock of black cloth was worn instead. White shirt collars were also worn, and a dozen of the same had to be produced at a kit inspection.

The last issue of this uniform[1] was made in 1838, but was worn until 1839, when a blue uniform was adopted.[2] The head-dress, with a slight alteration, continued in use until 1846.

King George IV. left many of his musical instruments to Lord Bloomfield, and they were placed by him in the care of the R.A. Band,[3] 1831. There were two violoncellos, one (with a floral design underneath the finger-board) being a magnificent instrument, two violas (one nick-named " Brownie," and another purfled with ivory), both being very fine instruments. There was also a violin, of peculiar shape, the ribs being shaped similar to a guitar, light in colour, and purfled with ivory. With the exception of the latter, which disappeared about twenty years ago, these instruments are still in the catalogue of the band instruments.

On one occasion the band was engaged to play at a ball in the Victoria Gardens, and there being no ferry in those days, they had to cross the river in small boats. When some distance from the shore, something was discerned following in the

---

[1] There is a painting in the possession of the widow of the late James Lawson (Bandmaster of the Mounted Band, R.A.) of Corporal C. M. Smith, of the R.A. Band, in this white uniform. There is also a reproduction of it in the R.A. Institution.

[2] *R.A. Institution Proceedings*, Vol. xiv.

[3] *England's Artillerymen.*—BROWNE, 1865.

wake of the boat, and at the same time the 'cello player missed his instrument. Hurriedly they pulled back to the object. It was the old " Bloom-field " 'cello, which had fallen overboard whilst they were entering the boat at the landing stage.

In 1831, His Majesty King William IV. visited Woolwich to launch H.M.S. " Thunderer." The R.A. Band, which was in attendance, so greatly attracted his attention, that in less than a week it was commanded to attend the Royal palace, where His Majesty personally complimented Mr. McKenzie, declaring that the Queen was especially delighted with the performances of the band. It was afterwards in frequent attendance at his palace.[1]

His Majesty offered to present the band with a pair of sterling silver kettledrums, but the drums when finished were only of copper, and handsomely painted. The King was so disappointed that he presented the officers with a superb candelabra. The drums, measuring thirty-two inches and thirty-five inches, were beautifully enamelled, bearing the Royal arms in gold, and superscribed :—

PRESENTED BY HIS MAJESTY WILLIAM IV.,
1833.

There is no record of any public ceremony at the presentation of these drums, as in the case of both regiments of Life Guards, who received theirs in 1831. But it is believed that they first made their appearance during one of the visits to the Royal

[1] *England's Artillerymen.*—BROWNE. 1865.

palace. The officers were presented with their piece of plate on the 8th August, 1833.

These drums were in continual use as orchestral drums[1] for over thirty years, and now rest in the Royal Artillery Institution, Woolwich; although in a deplorable condition, battered and bruised, most of the once magnificent enamel having disappeared, yet they are still preserved as a memento of the patronage and goodwill of William IV.

On the 23rd December, 1834, a grand performance of Handel's "Messiah" was given at the Royal Artillery Chapel[2] by the R.A. Band, assisted by several officers and local talent, in all nearly one hundred and thirty performers. The chorus numbered seventy-two, the solos being sustained by Miss Bruce, Mr. E. Seguin, the celebrated basso from Covent Garden, and Mr. Handel Gear. The orchestra, under the direction of Mr. McKenzie, the bandmaster, consisted of :—

First Violins	...	11	Oboes	...	2
Second Violins	...	10	Cornos	...	2
Tenors ...	...	5	Trombas	...	2
Violoncellos	...	9	Trombones	...	3
Double Bass	...	5	Serpent	...	1
Flutes ...	...	2	Ophicleide	...	1
Bassoons	...	2	Double Drums ...		1

Several eminent performers played in the orchestra on this occasion, notably Mr. C. Ashley, the celebrated 'cellist; Mr. Howell, the well-known

[1] The performer on these drums was Musician Job Carter, a very clever player, who taught Chipp, the celebrated *timpani* of the Italian Opera, the father of Dr. Edmund Chipp, of Ely, who, with his brother, played at the early R.A. Concerts.

[2] This old building was originally the Officers' Mess from about 1784 to 1802, when the present mess-rooms were taken into use; the old rooms being converted into a chapel, and in 1863 into a theatre.

double bass; Mr. Pattie and Mr. Hoff, Royal
Academicians. Among the officers who assisted
may be mentioned Dr. Kenning, M.D., Major Paddy,
Captain Wright, Dr. Colchester, M.D., and Lieut.
Thorndike.[1]

Sir George Smart and Sir John Stevenson were
present, and paid a very handsome compliment to
the performance. Sir John Stevenson invited
Mr. McKenzie and Bombardier Reeves, of the
R.A. Band, to join him at a musical party, where
they sang glees, etc., with him.[2]

Bombardier John Sims Reeves was the principal
bass vocalist of the band. He was the son of a
coachbuilder, and born at West Bromwich in 1791.
When eighteen years of age he joined the Marines,
but not liking that branch of the service, his friends
purchased his discharge. In 1815 he again enlisted,
this time in the Royal Horse Artillery. Here he
was noticed by Dr. Kenning, M.D., of that branch
(an excellent violinist), who had heard him sing,
and recommended him to Mr. McKenzie as a
valuable acquisition to the singing class. He was
accordingly transferred to the band, where his
superior attainments soon brought him to notice,
and he became the solo bass vocalist, playing the
bassoon and violin as well. Later he was appointed
to church clerk,[3] and, by virtue of this office,

[1] The late General Daniel Thorndike, R.A., grandfather
of Mr. Herbert Thorndike, the well-known singer.

[2] *England's Artillerymen.*—BROWNE, 1865.

[3] It was his duty as church clerk to announce the
anthem from the clerk's desk, and would frequently have to
rush away to the music gallery, where the band (for there
was no organ) and choir sat, to sing the bass solos.

occupied quarters in rear of the Artillery Chapel.[1] Here, on the 26th September, 1818, his wife Rosina gave birth to a son, called after his father, John, but known to the wide world as Sims' Reeves, "the finest tenor in Europe."

Unfortunately, this does not agree with the various biographies of our great singer, in which he is said to have been born at Shooters' Hill, Kent, on October 21st, 1822.[2] This is but a poetic flight from the R.A. Barracks, for we have the certificate of his baptism in the register at Woolwich Church, which avers that he was born in 1818 at New Road, which is true, for New Road reaches to the corner of the barracks where he was born. Reference to the register of 1822 brings no refutation, but confirmation strong, for we find that on October 20th, 1822, the tenor's sister, Harriet, was born at the R.A. Barracks the day before that which her brother John, otherwise Sims, thought he was born on Shooters' Hill.

In 1888 Sims Reeves published his autobiography,[4] and compromises matters somewhat by saying he was born in 1821, a year earlier than other accounts. But it was not until 1898, when a testimonial benefit

[1] Afterwards the R.A. Theatre. The house still remains, and the rooms occupied by Musician Reeves were on the upper floor.

[2] This was his father's second name, and he adopted it, we believe, after his return from Italy. At his first appearance in Aberdeen, in September, 1843, he was announced as Mr. John Reeves.

[3] *Dictionary of Music and Musicians*, by SIR GEORGE GROVE (1883); *The Life of Sims Reeves*, by SUTHERLAND EDWARDS, etc., etc.

[4] *The Life of Sims Reeves*, written by himself, 1888.

was contemplated for the veteran tenor, who was eighty years old in the September of that year, that he consented to the announcement[1] that he was born in 1818.

When only nine or ten years old Sims Reeves sang in the R.A. Band choir,[2] and in the performance of the " Messiah " in 1834, before mentioned, both his and his father's name appear in the list of the chorus.[3] Being rather promising, application was made for his enlistment, with another boy, the son of the band sergeant, but owing to some others having a prior claim (being orphans) their enlistment was delayed. When permission was granted, Bombardier Reeves informed the bandmaster that a clergyman at Footscray, having taken notice of his son, he thought he would be able to do better for him. Regarding his career, little requires to be said ; his fame is known to every intelligent lover of song in, we may say, all English-speaking lands.

He only once visited his native place, and sang at the Town Hall, William Street, where he had an enthusiastic reception. During this visit he had an interview with his old master, Mr. McKenzie. He died at Worthing, 25th October, 1900.

His father, Corporal John Reeves, will be long remembered both as a splendid singer and a good instrumentalist, whilst some manuscript music, still

[1] *British Musician*, July, 1898.

[2] *England's Artillerymen.*—BROWNE, 1865.

[3] This programme is in the possession of W. T. Vincent, Esq., the author of the *Records of Woolwich*, to whom I am greatly indebted for information.

preserved, bears testimony to his superiority as a penman. He took his discharge in 1838, with a very small pension, and took over the clerkship at a church at North Cray, his other son, Harry, singing in the choir. He died in November, 1860, at Footscray.

We must mention here the name of another distinguished R.A. Bandsman, who won honour in the more serious side of a soldier's life—on the field of battle. This was Andrew Henry, v.c., who served in the R.A. Band for some little time as a trumpet player, but early in the "forties" he transferred to the ranks. He served with great distinction in the Crimean War, being present at the battles of Alma and Inkerman. At the latter, whilst a sergeant in G Battery, Second Division, he defended his guns, almost single-handed, against overwhelming numbers, with the greatest tenacity; receiving no fewer than twelve bayonet wounds. In April, 1857, he received a commission in the Land Transport Corps, and on the 26th June, Her late Majesty Queen Victoria decorated him with the Victoria Cross, being the second one in the Royal Artillery to receive the coveted distinction. In November, 1859, he was promoted to captain in the Coast Brigade, R.A. He died suddenly at Devonport on the 14th October, 1870, and was buried at St. Mary's, Woolwich. His portrait appears in *Heroes of the Victoria Cross* (London, 1895), and a full description of his gallantry is recorded in *England's Artillerymen* and Kinglake's *Crimean War*.

At the Coronation Procession of Queen Victoria,

June, 1838, the R.A. Band was stationed in front of the Ordnance Office in Pall Mall.

The establishment of the band in 1839 was :—

```
1 Master
1 Sergeant
2 Corporals
4 Bombardiers (paid as Musicians)
14 Musicians
19 Bandsmen (paid as Gunners)
7 Boys (paid as Drummers)
——
48
```

The instrumentation consisted of :—

Piccolo	... 1	Trombones	...	4
Flutes	... 2	Ophicleide	...	1
Oboes	... 2	Bass Horns[3]	...	2
E flat Clarionets	... 3	Serpents	...	2
B flat Clarionets[1]	... 14	Tenor Drum	...	1
Bassoons	... 4	Side Drum	...	1
Trumpets	... 4	Bass Drum	...	1
Cornets	... 3	Cymbals	...	1
French Horns[2]	... 2			——
				48

This included seven boys who, only being learners, did not play with the band, which would reduce the number to forty, exclusive of the bandmaster. This had been the strength of the band for many years ; in fact, they earned an unpleasant soubriquet in consequence of this number. It happened during the reign of William IV., when the band was in great demand at the Royal palace. Its performances being usually at night time, it became necessary to provide the musicians with candles for their music desks, which were supplied by the Royal household. These were very superior wax candles, and the musicians came to look upon them as their per-

[1] Including the bandmaster, who invariably played with the band, and kept time by nodding his head and stamping. In the orchestra he conducted with his bow, à la Strauss.

[2] Natural or hand horns.

[3] These were really bass ophicleides.

quisites, and after each performance the partly-
used candles were appropriated for the sole purpose
of illuminating their rooms in barracks, which at
this time were lit up with candles. Then came the
order from the Royal household requesting the
musicians to leave the "very superior" wax
candles in their places. When this little episode
became known in Woolwich, the bandsmen were
immediately dubbed "The Forty Thieves."

The names of some of the solo performers in the
R.A. Band at this period occur in a poem entitled
"The Barrack Field," which appeared in the
Kentish Independent, August, 1887 :—

> "Again on the parade we stand
> To hear the Sunday evening band."
>
> * * * *
>
> "Do I remember? Yes, I do,
> Mackenzie,[1] Smith,[2] and Collins[3] too,
> And Harry Lawson,[4] Bill Devine,[5]
> While lesser stars around them shine.
> Tall Chew,[6] Ben Suffrien,[7] Billy Aitken,[8]
> Soul moving, stirring, spirit waking,
> With many others if I'd time
> I'd celebrate in rugged rhyme.
> Some grand descendants now adorn
> The laurels won and ably worn,
> And spread the fame throughout the land
> The ancient worthies of the band."

[1] The bandmaster.
[2] Band corporal and solo horn.
[3] Band sergeant and solo E flat clarionet.
[4] Solo cornet ; afterwards bandmaster of the Royal
Horse Artillery (*see* Chap. VII.).
[5] A very fine flute player ; afterwards bandmaster, 4th
Light Dragoons, 1842-67. The bandmaster of the 4th King's
Own from 1831-9 was George Coleman, also from the R.A.
Band.
[6] Bass trombone.
[7] Solo flute ; afterwards bandmaster, 17th Lancers.
[8] Piccolo.

Among these ancient worthies were musicians of considerable ability, but their talents were but little known and appreciated by the general public, for indeed the band rarely performed out of Woolwich, except on duty. Owing mainly to there being no railway to London, engagements were few and far between, except perhaps for the leading players, who alone could supplement their meagre pay by local " business " ; even these were fulfilled in a surreptitious manner as at this period the band had not the privilege of wearing plain clothes.

No one of importance, however, visited Woolwich without hearing the band at the R.A. concerts held in the Officers' Mess, the programmes of which invariably included an instrumental solo. Among the most notable performers may be mentioned John Wilkinson[1] and James Prendergrast, the solo violin and solo 'cello. The " lions " of the band were, however, among the brass—Henry Lawson[2] and William Keir,[3] the solo cornet and solo (slide) trumpet, both very fine performers, who frequently played brilliant duets by Labitzky and others.

The other soloists were : oboe, S. Devine ; clarionet, W. Collins, jun.[4]; bassoon, James Collins[5]; trombone, R. Warren.[6]

---

[1] Became bandmaster of the Royal Naval School, Greenwich.

[2] *See* Chap. VI.

[3] Afterwards regimental trumpet-major, R.A.

[4] *See* Chap. IV.

[5] IBID.

[6] Afterwards fife-major, R.A., and bandmaster, Forfar and Kincardine Artillery.

About this time a bassoon player named Riddle, who had been in the band since childhood, applied for his discharge and was refused. He thereupon appealed to the Master-General, stating that he had never been " sworn in." After some enquiry, it was found that no less than seventeen of the band had not taken the customary oath, and when required to do so many refused and were discharged. Among them was Mr. McCombie, afterwards band-master to the Viceroy of India.[1]

In September, 1843, Colonel Drummond died. He was very kind to the band, and, with Lord Bloomfield, did much to improve it. Colonel Samuel Rudyerd now took command of the band, but he died soon afterwards, when Colonel J. E. Jones, the Assistant-Adjutant-General, succeeded him, and the command of the band then became the duty attached to that appointment, until it was transferred to the Depôt Brigade, 1859.

Mr. McKenzie now having passed the age of sixty-five, he retired (January, 1845) with a pension of three shillings and a halfpenny per diem. The members of the band entertained him at a farewell dinner, held at the " Bull Tavern," when he was presented with a handsome silver snuff-box, suitably inscribed, which is now in the possession of the Lawson family. Mr. McKenzie was a great favourite with His Majesty William IV., and it was not at all an uncommon sight to see His Majesty offer his snuff-box to Mr. McKenzie.

Besides being an excellent singer, he was a capable

[1] *England's Artillerymen.*—BROWNE, 1865.

instrumentalist, and an indefatigable teacher. By his indomitable perseverance, he brought the band to such a pitch as to be unsurpassed in the country.[1]

He resided for many years with his son, a music-seller, at 17, Thomas Street, Woolwich, where he had a fine collection of stringed instruments, and occupied a little of his time in teaching. When he had turned eighty years of age he was still quite an active old man. Early in 1862 he was afflicted with paralysis, and he died on the 9th September, 1865.

William George Collins, a bombardier in the band, succeeded him as bandmaster.

[1] " It is satisfactory to note that the two best bands in England at this period, the Royal Artillery and the Cold-stream Guards, were controlled by Messrs. Mackenzie and Godfrey, whose names bespeak their nationality."— *Orchestral Times*, 1901.

From a painting in the R.A. Mounted Band Rooms.

CHAPTER IV.

1845-1854.

"I don't know what there was he couldn't do with yonder fiddle."
—FOC'S'LE YARNS.

"And he could strike a note that was sublime
With all the witchery of a tuneful lyre."
—ERIC MACKAY.

WILLIAM GEORGE COLLINS was the eldest son of William Collins, the band sergeant, R.A., the founder of the Collins family, which became as popular in the Royal Artillery as the Godfreys did in the Guards, or the Winterbottoms in the Marines.

Robert Collins and his brother William, (sen.), began their career in the Royal Irish Artillery Band; the former in 1791, and the latter in 1799, and both transferred to the R.A. Band, 1802. Robert[1] became the fife-major, R.A., and was discharged in 1834. His son Samuel served in the band 1817-60, and was discharged as band sergeant. William became the band sergeant in 1837, and was discharged in 1843. He was for many years

[1] His great-grandson, Stuart (Dick) Collins, was the last of the family to serve in the band. He took his discharge after seven years' service in 1891.

conductor of the Woolwich Harmonic Society,[1] and died in 1854, leaving seven sons and three daughters, all of whom were educated in the musical profession. Four of the sons served in the Royal Artillery—William, James and Frederick joining the band; the other, George, afterwards became trumpet-major and bandmaster of the Royal Horse Artillery.[2]

James joined the band in 1834, and became the solo 'cello, and was later appointed fife-major, R.A., and afterwards drum-major, R.A. About 1859, he became bandmaster of the Antrim Rifles, and died in 1865. His eldest son, William, was for many years band sergeant, Royal Engineers, and another son served in the R.A., as did also a daughter— a regimental schoolmistress.

Frederick joined the band in 1839, and became the solo viola; he was discharged as corporal in 1859, and became bandmaster of the Northumberland Militia Artillery.

William George Collins, the subject of this chapter, was born at Woolwich in 1815, and in November, 1825, enlisted in the band. Under the care and tuition of his father and Mr. McKenzie, he made great progress and was promoted to

---

[1] At the first public concert of this Society at the Harmonic Hall, Powis Street, on the 22nd February, 1841, out of the orchestra of twenty-one, twelve belonged to the R.A. Band, besides three in the chorus (*Records of Woolwich* —VINCENT). The present Woolwich Orchestral Society is conducted by Sidney Horton, Esq., late of the R.A. Band, in which he served from 1871 to 1881. He is a violinist and pianist of considerable ability, and played violin and piano concertos at the R.A. Concerts.

[2] *Jackson's Journal*, Feb., 1854.

bombardier, being solo clarionet in the military band, and one of the leading first violins in the orchestra.

He then turned his attention to composition, and studied under James Harris, Esq., Mus. Bac., Oxon.,[1] with whom he was a great favourite. On the retirement of Mr. McKenzie in 1845, he became "Master of the Band." Before he was appointed, however, he was subjected to a severe examination held at Blackheath, before Sir Henry Bishop, Cipriani Potter—the President of the Royal Academy of Music, and other eminent musicians, and passed with great credit, much to the chagrin of his numerous opposers, amongst whom were Lord Bloomfield and other influential officers, who, however, sensibly and honourably bowed to the decision of the appointed examiners.[2]

Collins was very popular, and Mr. Lawson states that on the day of his examination the members of the band threw old boots after him for good luck as he left the band rooms.[3] The appointment of so young a man of Mr. Collins' talent was very opportune. He at once set to work to infuse a vigorous style of playing into the band, more in accordance with the spirit of the age than the quiet, easy performances of bygone days. Mr. Collins was greatly assisted in this measure, as many of the older members took their discharge; younger men filling their places.

[1] *History of the Sappers and Miners.*—CONNOLLY.
[2] *England's Artillerymen.*—BROWNE, 1865.
[3] *Music and Musicians.*—MARR, 1887.

Mr. Collins organised concerts in the town, which were a great success. The following is a programme[1] of one given at the Theatre Royal, Beresford Street, on the 15th December, 1846, at which Miss Dolby, afterwards known as Madame Sainton-Dolby, the celebrated contralto, was engaged as vocalist:—

PROGRAMME.

PART I.

Sinfonia ...	"Alla Turca" (first movement) ...	Romberg
Chorus	"The Tempest : ' Around, around we pace ' "	Purcell
Recit. ed Aria ...	"A te riedo" ...	Mercadante
	Miss Dolby	
Waltz	"Emilie"	Collins[2]
Cavatina	"This heart by woe o'ertaken" (Maritana)	Wallace
	Mr. Wilkinson, R.A. Band	
Quartett ...	"What phrase sad and soft"	Sir H. Bishop
Song ...	"Oh, Araby!" (Oberon) ...	Weber
	Miss Dolby	
Solo Violin	"Sixth Air"	De Beriot
	Mr. Wilkinson, R.A. Band	
Overture		Collins[3]

PART II.

Overture	"William Tell"	Rossini
Scena ...	"All is lost" (Sonnambula) ...	Bellini
	Mr. Wilkinson, R.A. Band	
Solo Cornet à Piston	"The Banks of Allan Water"	B. Lee
	Mr. James Lawson, R.A. Band	
Ballad	"Primroses deck the bank's green side"	Linley
	Miss Dolby	
Solo Flute	"Original Air" ...	Richardson
	Mr. Bellingham, R.A. Band	
Trio	"Turn an old Time" (Maritana) ...	Wallace
	Miss Dolby, Messrs. Wilkinson and Browning, R.A. Band	
Quadrille	"British Navy"	Jullien
Polka	"Comic American"	Jullien

[1] In the writer's possession.
[2] The bandmaster. R.A.
[3] IBID.

At this time the band was recruited from young boys, as a rule only nine or ten years old, mostly "sons of the regiment," who were considered elegible before all others, although a few came from the Duke of York's School,[1] Chelsea, and the Royal Naval School, Greenwich, but always after a very careful selection. The singing-master taught them to sing, and prepared them for the soprano department of the band choir. Their general education was well looked after, and in the summer they attended school before breakfast, 6.0 to 7.30 a.m:, and again in the afternoon for an hour; they attended all the practices, both military and orchestral.

The daily routine of the band was a short practice (military) before "guard-mounting," which they attended with the Royal Marine Band. It was a very imposing affair. The guard was drawn up on the Barrack Field about 10.30 a.m. and inspected by the field officer of the day. The band then marched down the line playing a slow march, and returned playing in quick time.

The Guards then marched off, one party to the Arsenal, and the other to the Dockyard. The R.A. Band played the Arsenal guards to their post, and a selection of music was performed in the Dial Square whilst the old guards were being relieved.

---

[1] This institution played no small part in the progress of military bands in the early years of the last century. It turned out some of the finest clarionet players of the day. The bandmaster of the school was a Mr. Blizzard, a Waterloo veteran, noted for his purity of tone and style, which he imparted to his pupils, among them Lazarus, the finest clarionettist England has produced.

They were then played back to barracks, which they reached before twelve noon.

In the afternoon there was an hour's practice for the young members, which completed the musical duties of the day, except for the Thursday mess-nights, when the band performed from 9.0 to 10.0 p.m. In the winter there were the weekly orchestral and vocal concerts, known as the R.A. Concerts, also held in the Officers' Mess, on Tuesdays at 2.0 p.m.,[1] and in the summer there was the usual "playing-out" on the Barrack Field, generally two days in the week, morning and afternoon.

On Sundays, after the church parade, the band (orchestral)[2] played in the Artillery Chapel (afterwards the R.A. Theatre), for there was no organ.

> " The chapel where we're bound."
>
> * * *
>
> " Now, bandsmen play the soldiers in."
>
> * * *
>
> " They sing the ' Tate and Brady ' psalms,
> And praise with trumpets and with shawms."
>
> * * *
>
> " Anon the pealing anthem's swelling
> With grand effect ' The Heavens are Telling '
> With drum and oboe, brass and string,
> The sacred place is echoing."
> —*The Barrack Field.*

The choir was also furnished by the band, who occupied the centre of the upper gallery, flanked on

---

[1] There is evidence that in 1835 these were held on Fridays at 1 p.m.

[2] Generally string and wood-wind instruments ; brass only occasionally.

either side by the children from the regimental schools. A portion of the band also attended the afternoon service, under the direction of the band sergeant. Elaborate musical services were frequently given, and the performance of Kent's, Handel's and Mendelssohn's anthems by the band have been the admiration of the inhabitants of Woolwich for many years. Before a choir was established in this church, the only music performed there, was a voluntary, which was played upon wind instruments.[1]

In these days there was little or no printed music for the military band, except that occasionally an officer would bring some over from France or Germany, which was generally for instrumentation peculiar to continental bands, and useless until re-arranged. Those regiments that had bandmasters capable of composing and arranging were the best off, but their manuscripts were jealously guarded, and all sorts of expedients were resorted to for the purpose of replenishing the regimental music library.[2] If two regiments met, and their band-masters were friendly, they looked over each other's repertoire, and made exchanges, the bandsmen being set to work copying as fast as they could.[3]

---

[1] *England's Artillerymen.*—BROWNE, 1865.

[2] A story is told of a bandsman of the 4th (King's Own) Regiment, named Walthier, who, like Mozart in the Papal Chapel, could write music as he heard it, being set to work to secure a piece belonging to another band that was jealously guarded. He attended several performances, and succeeded so well that some men of the other band were charged with supplying the copies.

[3] In the R.A. Band two copyists were kept constantly employed.

These little amenities rarely extended beyond marches and light compositions. But the R.A. Band was better off than these; for, having a fine orchestra, playing the best music of the day, the bandmaster was able to arrange such music for the military band.

The first printed music for military bands published in England was issued by Messrs. Wessel between 1830 and 1840, but the circulation was limited, and the arrangement theoretical rather than practical. The first really effective arrangement for a military band published in London was by Herr C. Boosé, bandmaster of the Scots Fusilier Guards, who issued a selection from Verdi's opera, "Ernani," in 1845. It was soon taken up by Messrs. Boosey and Co., who undertook the production of a military band journal, appointing Herr Boosé sole editor.

The uniform worn by the R.A. Band at this period (1847)[1] was introduced in 1839, with the exception of the head-dress—the bearskin, which was adopted in 1846.

The bandmaster wore a double-breasted blue coatee with scarlet facings; the collar, cuffs and skirts being heavily laced with gold lace, and gold bullion epaulettes; dark blue trousers with two-

---

[1] From a portrait of W. Collins, bandmaster, R.A., in the possession of the R.A. Mounted Band, and also from a coloured photograph of Musician George Browning, kindly lent to the writer by his son, R. W. Browning, late bandmaster, Devon Artillery Militia and 2nd Devon Volunteers. A representation of a musician at this period is given in the *Records of Woolwich*, and also in an engraving, by Ranwell, of a review at the R.M. Academy, Woolwich (1840).

MUSICIAN,

ROYAL ARTILLERY BAND,

1847.

. . . . rarely extended beyond
. . . . compositions. But the R.A.
. . . . than these; for, having a fine
. . . . . playing the best music of the day, the
. . . . was able to arrange such music for
. . . .

. . . printed music for military bands pub-
. . . . was issued by Messrs. Wessel
. . . . 1810, but the circulation was
. . . . the arrangement theoretical rather than
. . . . . . The first really effective arrangement
. . . . military band published in London was by
. . . C. Boosé, bandmaster of the Scots Fusilier
. . . . who issued a selection from Verdi's opera,
". . . . ." in 18-5. It was soon taken up by
. . . . . . and Co., who undertook the pro-
d. . . . of a military band journal, appointing
Herr Boosé sole editor.

The uniform worn by the R.A. Band at this
period (1847)[1] was introduced in 1839, with the
exception of the head-dress—the bearskin, which
was adopted in 1846.

The bandmaster wore a double-breasted blue
coatee with scarlet facings; the collar, cuffs and
skirts being heavily laced with gold lace, and gold
. . . . epaulettes; dark blue trousers with two-

. . . portrait of W. Collins, bandmaster, R.A., in the
. . . of the R.A. Mounted Band, and also from a
. . . photograph of Musician George Browning, kindly
. . . the writer by his son, R. W. Browning, late band-
. . . Devon Artillery Militia and 2nd Devon Volunteers.
. . . . of a musician at this period is given in the
. . . . of . . . wich, and also in an engraving by Ranwell,
of a review of the R.M. Academy, Woolwich (1840).

MUSICIAN,
ROYAL ARTILLERY BAND,
1847.

inch gold lace stripes. The bearskin busby was of great size, with a plume of scarlet feathers on the left side, which encircled the top.

The non-commissioned officers, musicians, etc., wore a similar coatee, except that it was laced with half-inch gold lace, and smaller epaulettes. Trousers of dark blue[1] with a two-inch gold lace stripe for the sergeant, and scarlet cloth stripes for the remainder. They also wore the bearskin, with a short horse-hair plume of scarlet on the left side.

The boys wore the same as above, except that the lacing and epaulettes were of yellow worsted.

In undress[2] the bandmaster wore a dark blue frock coat, the front of which was laced with six rows of black braid, collar and cuffs laced with the same. The non-commissioned officers, musicians, etc., wore a dark blue shell jacket with fourteen small buttons down the front, scarlet collar, the back seams being piped with scarlet. The band sergeant's jacket was similar, except that it was laced with gold.

The forage cap was of dark blue, with a wide crown, and patent leather peak, scarlet cloth band and scarlet piping round the seams.[3] The bandmaster and band sergeant wore gold lace bands.

At this period the band carried no card cases;

[1] Light blue trousers were abolished in 1847, and dark blue substituted.

[2] The band had to pay for their undress uniform.

[3] In 1852 the forage cap was changed to one with a soft crown and gold lace band. About 1861 a cap similar to that worn at present was introduced.

the music for marching, etc., had to be committed
to memory.

Fixed regimental marches were unknown at this
time. Some corps certainly had traditional marches,
which they held most sacred[1]; but others played
certain tunes because the colonel's wife liked the
air, or perhaps because the colonel fancied the men
marched better to it than any other. It was considered the duty of a new bandmaster to compose
or select the regimental marches. In the early
years of the last century the R.A. Band played a
march composed by Mr. McKenzie, the bandmaster,
which was replaced by one composed by the succeeding bandmaster, Mr. Collins. The autograph
score of the latter is in the writer's possession,
which is dated 22nd July, 1848. But these were
slow marches. There were no fixed regimental
marches until the War Office order of 1882,
prior to which the R.A. Band used several marches
for this purpose of marching past, viz. : the
" British Grenadiers," " I'm Ninety-five," " Highland Laddie," and " Garry Owen."

On one occasion, about forty years ago, the
Royal Artillery were being marched past on
Woolwich Common to the latter tune, when the
Duke of Cambridge kept beating time with his

---

[1] Among these may be mentioned, the march of the
" Green Howards " (19th Foot), which was presented to the
regiment whilst on a tour of service in Austria, 1742. The
29th Foot, now known as the Worcestershire Regiment,
have a march called the " Windsor," composed for them by
Princess Augusta, a daughter of George III. The 15th
Hussars march, " Elliott Light Horse," dates as far back
as 1780; and the 14th Foot have for over a century played
the well-known French revolutionary air, " Ca Ira."

cane and shouting "Faster, that band!" The
bandmaster, Mr. Smyth, coolly took out his watch
and, timing the march by the minute hand, made
no alteration. The order at that date was one
hundred and eight paces to the minute, but very
soon afterwards it was increased to one hundred
and sixteen, and recently to one hundred and
twenty.[1]

It would seem that the "British Grenadiers"
was considered the regimental march in the R.A.
quite fifty years ago, for it is introduced into
a galop entitled "The Royal Artillery," composed by the bandmaster, Mr. Smyth, about
1855. It was fixed as the regimental march for
the regiment in 1882. This fine old melody is
very old, and it is impossible to ascertain its date.[2]

[1] The slow time of the English marches was for several
centuries a subject of remark among foreigners. "It was
formerly in high estimation, as well abroad as with us,"
says HAWKINS (History of Music). "Its characteristic is
dignity and gravity, in which respect it differs greatly from
the French, ... which is brisk and alert." Sir Roger
Williams, a gallant soldier of Elizabeth's time, had a con-
versation with the French marshal, Biron, on the subject
of English marches. The marshal observed that the
English march was slow, heavy and sluggish. "That may
be true," answered Sir Roger, "but, slow as it is, it has
traversed your master's country from one end to the
other."

[2] It is to be found in different forms at different periods.
It certainly cannot (as far as its title is concerned) be older
than 1678, when the grenadier companies were first formed.
In Queen Elizabeth's virginal book the melody appears as
"Nancie"; and in another MS. of the same time, as "All
you that love good fellows, or the London 'Prentice." In
a Dutch publication of 1643 it is known as "Sir Edward
Noel's delight," and during the Civil War it appears as
"Prince Rupert's March." The modern version as played
by the band (published by authority, Boosey & Co.) is
in the key of B flat, and is slightly different to the old
melody given by Mr. Chappell (Popular Music in the Olden
Time), which notation is over a hundred years old.

Mr. Chappell, in his *Popular Music of the Olden Time*, says: "Next to the national anthems, there is not any tune of a more spirit-stirring character than the ' British Grenadiers,' nor is any one more truly characteristic of English national music."

Prior to 1859 there was a drum-major, fife-major, and a trumpet-major in the Royal Artillery, besides a trumpet-major in the Royal Horse Artillery. These appointments were invariably given to members of the R.A. Band; who, however, in later years, did not sever their connection altogether, but played with the band whenever their duties would permit. The drum-major and fife-major taught the corps of drummers and fifers,[1] which relieved the R.A. Band of much duty.

> " See trumpeters assemble near,
> And from their lips the blast blows clear;
>
> See drummers with the fifers come,
> And Carter with the massive drum;
> The grand drum-major first doth stalk,
> With gold-knobb'd stick and pompous walk,
> And, as he marches o'er the ground,
> He thinks he turns the world around."
> —*The Barrack Field.*

All these wore scarlet with blue facings, except in the Royal Horse Artillery, where they wore the same as the ranks. The drum-major was a gor-

---

[1] The "drums and fifes" was a very efficient band. They practised daily, Saturdays excepted, from 10.30 to 12 noon, in the Gymnasium (" Garrison Orders," 11-10-1856).

geous individual, and he marched at the head of
the R.A. Band.

His uniform was a scarlet coatee with blue
facings, the breast, skirts, collar and cuffs being
heavily laced with gold; trousers of light blue,
with gold lace stripes, and gold Austrian knots in
front. Over his left shoulder he wore his "sash of
office" of blue and gold, and a crimson sash round
his waist. His head-dress was an enormous bearskin busby with a waving plume of scarlet feathers,
on the right side, which encircled the top.[1]

The fife-major and the trumpet-major, R.A., wore
a similar uniform, with the exception of the head-
dress, which was the shako, as worn by the rank
and file, and without the Austrian knots on the
trousers, and smaller epaulettes.[2] The drummers,
fifers, and trumpeters, R.A., wore double-breasted
scarlet coatees with blue facings, with shoulder
wings and trimmings of yellow worsted. The
scarlet uniform was abolished in 1851, when blue
was substituted, the trimmings and lacing remaining the same.[3]

The drum was discarded as a signal or duty
instrument in 1848,[4] the trumpet and bugle being
retained. But at Woolwich an efficient band of

[1] From a coloured print of the drum-major, R.A. (*circa*
1840), which hangs in the R.A. Band Reading Room.

[2] From a photograph of the Fife-Major, R.A., in the
possession of Mrs. Lawson.

[3] *History of the Dress of the R.A.*—MACDONALD.

[4] *Artillery Regimental History.*—MILLER.

drums and fifes was maintained until 1856,[1] when it was converted into a bugle band (*see* Chap. VIII.). The ranks of drum-major and fife-major continued until the introduction of the brigade system in 1859.

From 1859, the leader of the bugle band—James Lawson—was borne on the establishment of the regiment as the drum-major, although he did not march at the head of the R.A. Band. The title, drum-major, was dropped in April, 1865, when he was styled "master of the bugle band," although he continued to draw his pay as drum-major of the regiment until 1882. In December, 1859, an attempt was made to revive the glories of a marching drum-major, and the appointment was given to Bombardier James Lowrie,[2] but he gave up the position early in 1860. He was the last drum-major in the Royal Artillery. His uniform was a dark blue tunic with scarlet collar, the breast was laced with five rows of gold lace, the collar, cuffs, and back seams being also laced with gold. Trousers of dark blue with two inch gold lace stripes. His sash was scarlet, trimmed with gold. His head-dress was a bearskin, similar to that worn by the ancient worthies of that office. His entire uniform, and the staff,[3] which was used by many of his pre-

---

[1] The last reference to the drums and fifes occurs in the band accounts for 1856-7, where the drum-major is allowed five pounds for " providing music for the flutists " (*sic*).

[2] The present Lieut.-Colonel J. Lowrie, J.P., late commanding the 2nd Middlesex Artillery Volunteers.

[3] It may be of interest to note that perhaps the oldest drum-major's staff in existence is preserved at the Armoury House, Finsbury. It belongs to the Honourable Artillery Company, and was presented to them by its treasurer, Sir Mathew Andrews, in 1679.

decessors, are still preserved in the R.A. Institution.

The establishment of the R.A. Band[1] in 1849 was :—

    1 Master
    1 Sergeant
    2 Corporals
    8 Acting Bombardiers (paid as Musicians)
    12 Musicians
    19 Bandsmen (paid as Gunners)
    6 Boys (paid as Drummers)
    ——
    49

The following is a programme of a Royal Artillery concert, held in the Officers' Mess-room, on Tuesday, 27th February, 1849 :—

PART I.

Overture	...	...	"Zampa" ...	... ...	Herold
Solo and Chorus		"Come if you dare"	...	...	Purcell
Waltz ...	...	...	"Margarita"	...	D'Albert
Solo Clarionet	...	"11th Air Varie"	...	...	Berr
Galop di Bravura	...	...	... ...	...	Schulhoff

PART II.

Overture	...	...	"Anacreon"	...	Cherubini
Madrigal	...	"Soldiers brave and gallant be"		...	Gastoldi
Quadrille	...	...	"Flic Flac" ...	...	Schubert
Cavatina	...	"In questo semplice"	...	Donizetti
Polka ...	...	...	"Chinese Junk"	...	D'Albert

The principal instrumental performers at this period were: flute, Musician J. Bellingham; oboe, Bandsman V. Maine; B flat clarionet, Musician J. Farlie; B flat clarionet, Sergeant W. Newstead, sen.; bassoon, Musician R. Anderson; cornet,

[1] Quite half of the band resided out of barracks, and the remainder occupied quarters adjoining the Artillery Chapel (now the R.A. Theatre), on the top floor, the two small rooms serving as sleeping rooms, and the large room as a practice-room and mess-room. For many years the bandmaster's quarters were those on the top floor in the building (now a sergeants' mess) opposite the R.A. canteen.

Bombardier J. Lawson[1]; horn, Musician C. Gordon, sen.[2]; trombone, Bombardier T. Gilbertson[3]; ophicleide, Musician W. Lake[4]; violin, Bombardier S. Collins; viola, Musician F. Collins[5]; 'cello, Bombardier J. Collins.[6]

The first grand military concert ever given in this country took place in June, 1851, at Chelsea Hospital, in which the bands of the Royal Artillery, 1st and 2nd Life Guards, Royal Horse Guards, Grenadier, Coldstream, and Scots Guards, in all some three hundred and fifty performers, took part. The programme, which was performed on a raised platform in front of the portico in the great square, was divided into two parts, with seven pieces in each, and included :—march, *Le Prophète* ; overture, *Fest*, by Lulner ; overture, *Maritana* ; *Camp of Silesia* ; overture, *Euryanthe* ; Boisselots' *Ne touchez pas à la reine* ; *L'Huguenots* ; *Lucia de Lammermoor* ; *Nino* ; march from *Norma* ; quick step by Boosé ; waltzes by Karl Buller and D'Albert ; and Labitzky's famous *Quadrille of all Nations*. These were conducted by the respective bandmasters in turn.

The *Times*, commenting on the concert, said :—
" The execution of these pieces was so admirable, the ensemble so good, and the energy and decision

[1] Became bandmaster, Royal Artillery Mounted Band (*see* Chap. VIII.).
[2] For many years in the Carl Rosa Opera Orchestra.
[3] He was also the principal tenor vocalist, the principal bass vocalist being Bombardier G. Browning.
[4] Became bandmaster of several Metropolitan Police Bands.
[5] Became bandmaster, Northumberland Artillery (*see* Chap. IV.)
[6] Became bandmaster, Antrim Rifles (*see* Chap. IV.).

of the conductors so remarkable that the unequivocal satisfaction of the auditors was not to be wondered at. We only regretted that with such splendid means so little of real musical importance was effected. The overture to *Euryanthe* alone among the 14 pieces presented to the public was worthy of consideration as an artistic performance. Our military bands have reached a very high degree of perfection in regard to the mere talent of execution; but in other respects they have done little or nothing to assist the progress of the art. If the bandmasters who train them so zealously and well would endeavour to instil into them some notion of true music, instead of confining them almost wholly to the most ephemeral productions, their influence would be highly beneficial."

The R.A. Band was engaged at the ceremony of the planting of the first pillar at the Crystal Palace on the 5th August, 1852; they also fulfilled engagements at Cheltenham, Hatfield, Colchester, Ashford, Aylesbury, etc. In November, 1852, it was ordered to take part in the funeral procession of the Duke of Wellington, and played the funeral march from Mendelssohn's *Antigone*, and a movement from Spohr's symphony, *Die weihe der töne.*

It was taken to Brighton in December, 1853, by Captain (afterwards Lieutenant-General Sir David) Wood, R.H.A., "where its performances as a string band first elicited that commendation which has since been re-echoed throughout the length and breadth of the land."[1]

---

[1] *England's Artillerymen.*—BROWNE, 1865.

The following is an extract from the *Brighton Gazette* of that month :—

"This band, which we believe, never performed in Brighton before, is acknowledged to be the best in the service ; and for versatility of talent it is unrivalled : it contains in itself a brass (*military*) band, a stringed, and a vocal band. There is none to equal it ; and we can only imagine that it was brought to its present pitch of perfection by the indomitable perseverance of its talented conductor, Mr. Collins. If we had heard no other performance than the selection from " Lucrezia Borgia," it would have been sufficient to stamp our admiration of their playing. All the points were worked out with a master-hand and with much spirit, and at the same time evenness of tone : no single instrument was so far predominant as to pain even the critical ear by the circumstance of its being over-powering. The crescendos that we never heard excelled, if equalled, were beautifully worked up, and the subdued passages given with all that exquisite modulation that nothing but a thorough drilling under a first-rate master like Mr. Collins could effect. It was remarked by many in the room that this performance approached perfection as near as it possibly could be reached ; and we doubt not, if Donizetti could have heard this music handled by our artillery band, he would not say with many that the English were far behind the foreigners in their appreciation and performance of good music. We cannot let this opportunity pass without offering our meed of praise to the cornet player, Mr. Lawson, who is a second Kœnig on that

instrument. His solos were given with the utmost
purity of tone and taste; and we heard frequent
exclamations of—' Beautiful !' We shall probably
by some be thought too lavish in praise of this band ;
but we could not discover a single point with which
to find fault. Three vocal pieces were performed :
Sir Henry Bishop's glee, ' Blow, gentle gales,' the
serenade ' Sleep, gentle lady,' and the echo chorus
from Weber's ' Preciosa' ; the solo parts being sustained by Master W. Maine, Master J. A. Browne,[1]
Messrs. Gilbertson, Wells, and Smith. In the
serenade the treble of Master Maine was very
sweet, well in tune throughout, although we
understand his voice is breaking. The bass of
Mr. Joseph Smith was flowing and telling,
without any degree of harshness; the tenor of
Mr. Gilbertson was admirable, and the counter-
tenor, with a trifling exception, accorded well with
the other voices. At the close of the performances,
Mr. Collins was much complimented by several of
the company on the efficiency to which he had
raised his band, and by none more so than by the
Hon. Archibald Macdonald, ' father of the London
Catch Club.' The performers are for the most part
young men, and many of them mere boys, a circumstance which shows that greater credit is due
to the conductor."

The success of the band was such, that the best
engagements in Brighton for that and the following
seasons were sent to the R.A. Band. Local
musicians were naturally very indignant, and sar-

[1] Became bandmaster, Royal Horse Artillery.

castic remarks were made in some of the papers about the " soldier fiddlers." However, the band went annually to Brighton, and in 1866, in conjunction with Madame Liebhart, gave morning and evening concerts for an entire week.[1]

Between 1830 and 1860 a great many changes took place in military music. It was stated in the last chapter that bands were formed on their own model, using what instruments they liked ; consequently there was no common pitch, and it was almost impossible to combine several bands for united performances. It was William Wieprecht, a German, who was the first to clearly perceive the want of a complete reconstruction, and also to devise a plan of an instrumentation fixed according to artistic needs. His first attempt was to construct the modern brass band about 1828, when he introduced a complete family of valved instruments, comprised of E flat cornets, B flat cornets, B flat tenor horns, and euphoniums. Seven years later he designed the bombardon. In 1838 he was appointed director of the bands of the Prussian Guards, and from this time dates the gradual revolution in the organisation of the military bands in almost all European States, and formed the basis of our present military music.

---

[1] "The fullness of tone, without the slightest harshness, produced by this band is at once a proof that every instrument is under the fullest control of the performers. Added to this is the tenderness and artistic feeling displayed by the soloists, to say nothing of the exquisite colouring by the strictest attention to the piano crescendos and fortes of the composers, forming altogether an ensemble not hitherto realised here."—*Brighton Gazette*, 3-1-1867.

Then came Adolph Sax, who, like Wieprecht in Germany, created a revolution in French military music. He adapted the valve to all classes of brass instruments, which he called saxhorns, saxtrombas, saxtubas, etc., ignoring the fact that these instruments were known, although not in general use, long before his " inventions " were patented. These were almost immediately adopted in England under the names of saxhorns, althorns, euphoniums, and bombardons. The two latter seem to have been adopted first, and entirely superseded the tenor and bass ophicleides, bass horns and serpents.[1] Another invention of M. Sax, was the saxophone, which remains his most important discovery.

Nor had the brass family alone been improved upon. Boehm, Triebert, Klosé, and others, had greatly increased the executive capacity of the " wood wind " by their improvements and inventions.

British " crack " regiments, now at the zenith of their extravagance in military musical matters, spent enormous sums in purchasing instruments of the new type, for even at this date the rivalry between regimental bands was as keen as ever. But whatever may be said of such a system, it is undeniable that the musical results were in many cases notable, and the service could boast fifty years ago of many superior bands,[2] besides those of the Guards and Artillery.

[1] The last serpent player in the band was Bombardier G. Browning, and the identical instrument is still preserved in his family. It appears in the illustration facing page 90.

[2] *Military Music.*—KAPPEY.

In April, 1854, Mr. Collins, the bandmaster, R.A., took his discharge on a pension. He then became bandmaster of the Royal Bucks Militia, " which, from his peculiar fitness and attainments, became one of the best bands among the regular troops or militia in the kingdom."[1] On the disembodiment of the regiment, his engagement with Lord Carrington having ceased, his well-known reputation led to his instant appointment as Master of the newly-formed band of the Royal Engineers at Chatham (August, 1856), the first appointed in that corps.[2]

In this position he also achieved success, and it was he who established the string band in that corps.[3]

He retired in 1865 to Woolwich, and later removed to Torquay, where he died, 10th March, 1886, aged 71.[4]

Mr. Collins was a clever musician. Besides being an excellent clarionet player and a good violinist, he was an advanced theorist, and also an effective arranger for both military band and orchestra, but he was a very reserved man, who had been brought up in a narrow groove, bounded on every side by Woolwich, and was sadly wanting in tact and experience. That the officers of the

---

[1] *History of the Sappers and Miners.*—CONNOLLY.

[2] Prior to this, there had been a brass band in the corps, under the direction of Bugle-Major Youle.

[3] ROBERT MARR, in his *Music for the People* (1889) gives Mr. J. Sawerthal the credit of this, which is an error. (See also *History of the Sappers and Miners.*—CONNOLLY.

[4] His decease is recorded on the back of the tombstone of Ralph Bennett, 178 —, in Plumstead Churchyard.

Royal Engineers were well satisfied with him,
however, may be gathered from the fact of their
going to the same school for his successor,
Mr. William Newstead, jun., a sergeant in the
Royal Artillery Band. He was the eldest son of
the band sergeant, R.A., and was born at Woolwich
in 1826. In 1837 he joined the R.A. Band, and
was for many years the solo clarionet in the military
band, and one of the leading violins of the orchestra.
He became bandmaster, Royal Engineers, in 1865,
and remained with them until 1871. He died in
1875 as bandmaster of the Northampton Volunteers.[1] "Coming from a good school of music,
the first conductors were enabled to raise the band
[the Royal Engineers] to a high state of efficiency,"[2]
and they laid the foundations for the present famous
band of that corps.

James Smyth, the bandmaster of the 19th Regiment, succeeded Collins as bandmaster of the
Royal Artillery.

---

[1] His brother Henry also served in the R.A. Band, and
became bandmaster of the 106th Regiment. To this
gentleman I am greatly indebted for information.

[2] *Music and Musicians.*—MARR, 1887.

Photo by Cobb, Woolwich.

CHAPTER V.

1854-1881.

"Up from beneath his masterly hand in circling flight
The gathering music rose."
—HOMER (translated by SHELLEY).

"I am what I am because I was industrious; whoever
is equally sedulous will be equally successful."—BACH.

JAMES SMYTH was the son of a guardsman,
and was born in London, 18th March, 1818,
and baptised at St. James' Church, Piccadilly.
When he was quite young, his father was
promoted to the 19th Regiment, and his son was
taken into the regimental band. Under the care of
Mr. Brown, the bandmaster, an excellent musician,
he made rapid progress in every department. The
19th was one of the few line bands which had a
string band, and soon we find Corporal Smyth
first violin and solo clarionet. His abilities were
so marked that when Mr. Brown retired in 1841,
he was appointed bandmaster.

He saw much foreign service, being stationed at
Malta, Cephalonia, Corfu, West Indies and Canada.
At Montreal, where his string band was engaged
to furnish the orchestra for the Seguin Opera
Company, he made the acquaintance of one of the
prima donne of the company, an eminent contralto,
of the Royal Opera, Stuttgardt, whom he married.[1]

Arriving in England, the reputation of Mr. Smyth

[1] *British Musician*, Sept., 1898.

. . . . at
. . . . anada,
. . . . . . s engaged
. . . . Opera
. . . . . . of one of the
. . . . contralto,
Stuttgart, wh . . . he married.
. . . the reputation of Mr. Smyth

. . Sept., 1808.

Photo by Cobb, Woolwich.

JAM... ... ... a gentleman,
... ... 18th March, 1818,
... ... Green, Piccadilly.
... ..., his father was
promot... ... ..., and his son was
.ken i: ... ... under the care of
... B... ... ... excellent musician,
... ... department. The
... ... which had a
... ... Corporal Smyth
first vi... ... ... His abilities were
so marke... ... ... returned in 1841,
.e was a... ... ...

.He saw ... ... being stationed at
... Cey... ... ... West Indies and Canada.
... ... during that was engaged
... ... in the Seguin Opera
..pany, be... ... ... acquaintance of one of the
.. donne of t... ... ..., eminent contralto,
... Royal C... ... ..., whom he married.[1]
... ... portion of Mr. Smyth

... Music ... ... 8.

and his band increased, particularly at Plymouth, where the local Philharmonic Society was conducted by him. When the regiment left Plymouth, he was presented with a handsome silver salver by the society as a " mark of their appreciation of his talent, and of the zeal, energy and devotion " with which he had carried them through two important seasons—1851-2.

In 1853 the regiment went to Chobham Camp, and here the superiority of the band of the 19th became unpleasantly apparent. Lord Seaton invariably sent for it when the Queen or any distinguished visitors lunched with him, and on one occasion Mr. Smyth was highly complimented by Her Majesty, who sent an aide-de-camp to inform him that his conducting had been the means of producing a spirited and good performance[2]; also when the combined bands played (then quite a novel feature in the service) Mr. Smyth was usually selected to conduct them, until he (seeing the ill-feeling arising) suggested to the authorities that the different bandmasters should take this duty in turn.

When the Crimean War broke out the 19th was ordered to the seat of war, and the officers not wishing to part with their bandmaster, whom they could not take with them, promised him a commission as quartermaster; but the Commander-in-Chief would not sanction such an unprecedented appointment, as it was at that time.

In April, 1854, the mastership of the Royal

[2] *The Herald*, 20-8-1853.

Artillery Band became vacant, and Mr. Smyth applied for the position and was appointed.[1] He was surprised to find, however, that his pay would be less than one-half he had received in the 19th; for at this time there were only four bandmasters recognised in the Army Estimates, viz. : the "master" of the R.A. Band at five shillings and sixpence per diem, the "bandmaster" of the Royal Military Asylum, Chelsea, at six shillings per diem, "a sergeant acting as master of the band" at the Royal Military College, Sandhurst, at three shillings per diem, and "a sergeant of instruction in music," at fifty pounds per annum, for the Royal Hibernian School, Dublin; but the band of the Royal Artillery was the only *band* recognised in the Estimates, and payments were still granted for one band sergeant, two corporals and twenty musicians, besides the bandmaster, and one hundred pounds for instruments and music.

All other regimental bands were supported by a band fund, to which each officer had to subscribe, and could afford to pay their bandmasters from twelve and sixpence to one pound per diem. No such fund existed in the Royal Artillery, as their band was supported by the Government; so Mr. Smyth had to content himself with his bare pay. Yet he saw possibilities in such a position, and in less than two years he made it worth three hundred and sixty pounds per annum, exclusive of engagements.[2]

[1] His brother Thomas became bandmaster of the Royal Marines, Woolwich, soon afterwards.

[2] *R.A. Band Fund Accounts*, 1856-7.

During the summers of 1854-5-6 the R.A. Band was in frequent attendance at the Crystal Palace, including the " Grand Military Fête " on October 28th, 1854, and the Peace Festival on the 9th May, 1856, which was attended by Queen Victoria and the Prince Consort.

On the 26th December, 1854, the band gave its first orchestral concert in London at the Royal Panoptican (now the Alhambra), Leicester Square.[1]

In the autumn of 1855 a series of concerts were given in the north of England, at Durham, Sunderland and Newcastle. Seldom hearing any music of a higher class than that performed by the local bands, the people of the north were almost frantic with excitement at the performance of the band on this occasion, and frequent applications have since been made for them to visit that part of the country. These concerts were followed by others at Bath, Bristol, etc. This is probably the earliest notice of a military band going on a concert tour at any distance from headquarters.[2]

Mr. Smyth, however, had taken over the band under the most unfavourable circumstances. The officers to whom he was unknown, and the whole of the bandsmen, were to some little extent prejudiced against him ; for he was an infantry bandmaster, and the Royal Artillery for nearly half a century had boasted of bandmasters born and educated in the regiment.

However, by the following year he had quite

---

[1] *England's Artillerymen*—BROWNE, 1865.
[2] *British Musician*, Sept., 1898.

established himself with his officers, and they expressed their appreciation to the band commandant, who communicated the same to Mr. Smyth in the following :—

"D.A.G. OFFICE, WOOLWICH,
"11th August, 1855.

" MR. SMYTH,

"It will no doubt be gratifying to you to know that the talent you brought with you, on succeeding to the appointment of Master of the Royal Artillery Band, has so developed itself in the improvement of the band that the officers of the corps are much pleased, and many of them have expressed themselves in terms highly commendatory to your merits.

"H. PALLISER, Adj.-Gen., R.A."

Thus encouraged, Mr. Smyth induced the officers to increase the establishment of the band; and on the 1st January, 1856, it was ordered that the band should be increased to eighty[1] :—

```
 1 Master
 1 Band Sergeant
 3 Sergeants
 1 First Band Corporal
 1 Second Band Corporal
 2 Corporals
 4 Bombardiers
 4 Acting Bombardiers
16 Musicians
33 Bandsmen
14 Boys
──
80
```

Now we find a reversion of the feelings of the bandsmen towards Mr. Smyth. On the 11th January, 1856, they gave him a supper at the

[1] *England's Artillerymen.*—BROWNE, 1865.

"King's Arms Hotel," to publicly express their gratitude to him. Mr. McKenzie, the late bandmaster, R.A., was among the guests. The toast of the evening was :—"The health of Mr. Smyth, with heartful thanks to him for his successful exertions in bettering the position and prospects of the band."

Mr. Smyth's efforts for the good of the band never relaxed. The allowance from the Government, was found to be inadequate to meet the requirements of the band since the augmentation, so Mr. Smyth induced the officers to raise a band fund. This was established on the 25th January, 1856, to which each officer in the regiment had to subscribe two days' pay annually. This amounted in the first year to over one thousand pounds. The band now came under the care of a band committee, consisting of Colonel J. Bloomfield, president; Lieutenant-Colonel Charles Bingham, secretary and treasurer; Captain R. K. Freeth and Captain J. F. D'Arley Street, committee.[1]

It was now found that a considerable number of the instruments in use by the band were the property of the bandsmen, and out of the forty stringed instruments in use, only six belonged to the regiment; the remainder, with the exception of five lent by Lord Bloomfield, were the bandsmen's own property.[2] Many of the wind instruments

[1] R.A. Band Fund Accounts, 1856-7.

[2] The musicians were allowed a small sum for the expenses of strings, &c., called "string money," which was abolished in this year, strings being supplied by the Band Fund.

had from long use become utterly unserviceable, and there were still a few of the increased number of musicians without instruments. Arrangements were immediately made to procure new instruments from good makers in London, and during 1856-7 sixty-three wind and four stringed instruments were purchased. The committee next took into consideration the proposal of Mr. Smyth's, of granting an addition to the regimental pay of the band by an allowance from the band fund, intended to reward merit and talent, and as an inducement to young musicians, so as to apply themselves to their profession as to become efficient.[1] They resolved to grant an allowance to:—

(a.) "Soloists according to the importance of their respective instruments, and their efficiency in performing on them."

(b.) "Musicians, who, although not soloists, have by zeal and application to their profession, made themselves useful members of the band."[2]

The first band fund allowance was granted to:—

Master of the Band	6/6
Trumpet-Major (Solo Cornet)	3/-
Senior Sergeant (Leader of the Orchestra)	7½d.
Fife-Major (Solo Trombone)	8d.
Three Sergeants...	1/-
Corporals	1/1
Four Bombardiers	1/-
„ „ (Musicians)	1/1
Ten Gunners and Drivers	2/1

This band fund pay amounted for the first year to over three hundred pounds, and by the following

---

[1] *R.A. Band Regulations*, 1st April, 1856.
[2] *R.A. Band Fund Accounts*, 1856-7.

year Mr. Smyth induced the Band Committee to increase it to four hundred and fifty pounds per annum, but without taking any addition to his own salary.

In 1856 a new uniform was introduced for the band, and was taken into wear, May 29th.

The uniform of the non-commissioned officers and men was:—A dark blue tunic[1] with scarlet collar, the front being adorned with five rows of gold lace. The cuffs, back seams and the collar were laced with the same, the whole of this lace being traced on both edges. An embroidered lyre was worn on the forearm of each sleeve, a distinction never before or since conferred on a military band. An embroidered grenade was worn on each shoulder strap. The trousers were of dark blue, with two inch scarlet cloth stripes.

The head-dress was a black sable busby, with scarlet bag on the right ; and on the left side a gilt brass grenade, surmounted by a scarlet hackle feather plume, reaching to the top of the busby, and a patent leather chin strap.

The band sergeant wore the same as above, with the exception of the tunic, which had some additional lacing.[2] The boys wore a tunic similar to that worn by the regiment, only perfectly plain, with an embroidered lyre on each sleeve.

The bandmaster's tunic was totally different to the band. The front edges were laced with two-

---

[1] This tunic was the suggestion of Musician W. Lake, R.A. Band, who embodied his idea in a water-colour sketch, and suggested it to Mr. Smyth, who brought it to the notice of the officers.

[2] This was not adopted until 1864.

MUSICIAN,

ROYAL ARTILLERY BAND,

1856.

e being
e was
tton
and,
der
two

w, with
a gilt
ackle
busby,

e, with
e addi-
ar to
y plain,

rent to
th two

This tune was the W. Lake
B A Band, who composed sent
sted it to Mr Smith

was not adopted until

MUSICIAN,
ROYAL ARTILLERY BAND,
1856.

inch gold lace, the outer edge being handsomely traced. The cuffs and back seams were laced with one-inch gold lace, and the collar with half-inch gold lace. On the forearm of each sleeve was an embroidered device, consisting of a lyre, grenade, trumpets, drums, etc., and above this a gun and crown. He also wore a gold lace cross belt.

The bandmaster, band sergeant and sergeants wore gold lace stripes on the trousers, and the two former wore gold lace slung belts, with steel swords. The remainder of the band wore a strap underneath the tunic, with a frog of black patent leather, which protruded through an opening at the side of the tunic ; the sword was similar to that worn in 1847, only longer.

This uniform remained practically unaltered until 1879, when the head-dress was changed to a blue cloth helmet, with gilt brass mountings, similar to that worn by the officers, with the addition of a wreath of laurels, which encircled the front; from the ball at the top issued a waving plume of scarlet horsehair, which fell over the helmet, reaching to the bottom.

About 1882 the grenades on the shoulder straps of the tunic were abolished ; and with the bandmaster, gold twisted cords were substituted in the place of the cloth shoulder straps. The lyre and the chevrons were in future to be worn on the right arm only.[1]

The helmet was abolished in 1895, and a busby

---

[1] The embroidered ornaments on the bandmaster's sleeves were abolished about the same time.

similar to that worn in 1856 was adopted, except that the plume was higher, and a curb chain for the chin. This was again altered in 1899, the plume at the side being taken away, and one of the scarlet horsehair placed in front.

The instrumentation of the band in 1857 was[1] :—

MILITARY.

Flutes and Piccolo	...	2	Sopranos, E flat	...	2
Oboes	...	4	Fügel Horns, B flat	...	2
Clarionets, E flat	...	4	,, ,, E ,,	...	2
,, B ,, (1st)	...	10	French Horns ...	...	4
,, B ,, (2nd & 3rd)		12	Althorns	...	2
Saxophones, E flat	...	2	Trombones ...	...	4
,, B ,,	...	2	Euphoniums ...	...	2
Bassoons ...	...	4	Bombardons, E flat	...	4
Cornets	...	4	Drum, etc. ...	...	3
Trumpets	...	2			—
					71

ORCHESTRA.

First Violins ...	...	12	Bassoons	...	2
Second Violins ...	...	12	Cornets	...	2
Violas	...	5	Trumpets ...	...	2
'Cellos	...	4	Horns	...	4
Contra Basses ...	...	4	Althorn[2]	...	1
Flutes and Piccolo	...	3	Trombones ...	...	3
Oboes	...	2	Euphonium ...	...	1
Clarionets ...	...	2	Bombardon, E flat[3]	...	1
Saxophones ...	...	2	Drums, &c. ...	...	3
					—
					65

The vocal department consisted of :—

Soprano—Boys	...	18
Alto—Men	...	12
Tenor ,,	...	24
Bass ,,	...	24
		—
		78

[1] R.A. Band Fund Accounts, 1856-7.

[2] This instrument seems somewhat out of place in an orchestra, but it was utilised by Mr. Smyth for the performance of vocal solos in some of his admirable operatic selections, etc.

[3] The bombardon did the duties of the *tuba*.

With such a wealth of instrumentation, the performance of all works was possible. But it was far different with the line regiments, whose bands had suffered severely during the Crimean campaign ; for when this war broke out many regiments turned their bandsmen into the ranks.[1]

Those bands that were present in the Crimea, under the direction of their band sergeants (the bandmasters, being civilians in most cases, did not accompany them), were in a very poor plight. Attention was first called to the deplorable state of our military bands at the Queen's Birthday parade at Varna in 1854, where, before the staff of the allied armies, our bands struck up "God save the Queen," not only from independent arrangements, but in different keys.[2] It was much commented upon at the time, and the Duke of Cambridge was evidently much impressed, for one of his first orders when he became commander-in-chief was that the national anthem was to be played in B flat.[3]

The war at an end, attention was directed to our

---

[1] At the outbreak of the war the band of the 17th Lancers consisted of about twenty men, many of them foreigners, who claimed their discharge, whilst about three were turned into the ranks. (*Story of the 17th Lancers*— PARRY.)

[2] A similar incident occurred a year later, when Her Majesty Queen Victoria paid a visit to Shorncliffe Camp. (*Folkestone Chronicle*, 12-8-1885.)

[3] Even this was found to be insufficient, many bandmasters having inserted peculiar harmonies of their own, others having running bass parts, etc. It then became necessary to issue a regulation edition, that for the infantry being arranged by Mr. Dan Godfrey, bandmaster, Grenadier Guards, and that for cavalry bands by Mr. Waterson, 1st Life Guards.

bands. Mr. James Smyth, the bandmaster, R.A., with M. De Lara-Bright, an enthusiastic amateur at Sheffield, Herr Schallehn,[1] and others, urged upon the Duke of Cambridge and the Secretary of State for War the necessity of improving the position of bandmasters and bandsmen if we were to reach the standard of continental bands.[2]

They impressed upon the authorities that a musician was something more than a private soldier; that his pay should be increased, that he was worthy of promotion, that greater facilities should be given to further his musical education, and that he was capable of being trained as a bandmaster.

The immediate result was an official recognition of army bands by the establishment of a Royal Military School of Music at Kneller Hall, near Hounslow, on the 3rd March, 1857, under the fostering care of the Duke of Cambridge, the Commander-in-Chief. It began under the modest title of the "Military Music Class," and I believe employed a staff of four professors only, including the director of music, who was then called the "resident instructor." At first it was but a half-hearted affair, being supported entirely by regimental subscriptions.

The subscription from the Royal Artillery for the first year amounted to thirty-nine pounds.

[1] For some time bandmaster of the 17th Lancers, and Musical Director at the Crystal Palace. He became the Director of Music at the opening of the Royal Military School of Music.

[2] *British Musician*, Sept., 1898.

When the school opened, two boys were sent from the R.A.,[1] and they remained there for about two years. The report on their progress was not so satisfactory as was expected, and it was decided that, as the young members of the band had far better opportunities for instruction in the band than they could possibly receive at Kneller Hall (the Military School of Music), no more would be sent there for instruction.[2]

The Royal Artillery still continued, however, to subscribe most liberally towards the military music fund,[3] which supported the school, until 1865, when the band committee decided to withdraw their subscription, which was only just, considering the little benefit which the band derived from the school; but after taking into consideration the great boon which this institution was to other bands, the regiment agreed to allow thirty pounds per annum towards its maintenance.[4] Kneller Hall was taken over by the Government in 1875.

This institution has been a remarkable success, and the excellent condition of our military bands to-day is ample proof of the good work done at

---

[1] The first pupil sent to the school was George C. Smith, who was also the first pupil or student in the army to arrive there. He became quartermaster-sergeant of the band, and at present is the bandmaster of the 1st Lancashire Artillery Volunteers, etc.

[2] The total number of musicians of the R.A. Band trained as pupils at Kneller Hall is, I believe, only ten—1857, two; 1881, one; 1883, three; 1901, three; 1902, one.

[3] Up to 1865 the R.A. had contributed £375 towards this fund.

[4] Letter Books, R.A. Band Committee.

Kneller Hall. It has been the means of having an educated body of British bandmasters with a defined position, and providing promotion for a number of deserving military musicians, who hitherto had been kept out of the position by civilians, for the most part men from the continent. The Royal Military School of Music has, however, had nothing to do with the training or the present high state of efficiency of the Royal Artillery Band. None of its bandmasters have had any connection with the school, and the training of the band has always been, with the exception of the few already mentioned, entirely under the care and tuition of the bandmaster and his various subordinates. In fact, we may say that the reverse is the case, for both military music and Kneller Hall owe a great deal to the Royal Artillery Band. Apart from the exertions of Mr. Smyth for the advancement of military music, this band was one of the pioneers in the introduction of classical music in the military band. Moreover, the Directors of both the military and naval schools of music received their earliest tuition in the Royal Artillery Band.

The Director of Music at the Royal Military School of Music is Lieutenant Arthur J. Stretton. He was born on the 5th April, 1865, and joined the R.A. Band at Sheerness in 1875, being instructed by the bandmaster, Mr. Charles M. Glaysher. In October, 1882, he transferred to the R.A. Band at Woolwich, and in addition to the training he received in the band, he took lessons on the violin from the late J. T. Carrodus, and studied harmony and the piano under Dr. Warwick Jordan. He entered Kneller Hall as a student in 1891, and in September, 1893, was appointed bandmaster of the Cheshire Regiment. In March, 1896, he was the successful candidate for the position of Director of Music at the Royal Military School of Music, at which institution he had studied only three years before.

The present commandant of Kneller Hall is also from the "Royal Regiment." This is Colonel F. O. Barrington-Foote, for many years president and commandant of the R.A. Band at Woolwich. The late euphonium professor, Mr. Charles Cousins, was at one time in the R.A. Band, as was also Mr. Walter Hayward, the present oboe professor.

Mr. Edward E. Stretton, brother to the director at Kneller Hall, is the Director of Music at the Royal Naval School of Music. He served in the R.A. Band from 1886, and became bandmaster of the 1st York and Lancaster Regiment. In 1903 he was selected to direct the new school for naval bandsmen.

Some of the most prominent bandmasters in the service to-day have also served in the R.A. Band.

Mr. Albert J. Cunningham, who served in the R.A. Band, 1883-94, became bandmaster of the Royal Irish Rifles in 1896, and was appointed to the newly-formed Royal Garrison Artillery Band at Dover in 1903.

Mr. Robert G. Evans served in the band 1885-9, when he transferred to the Coldstream Guards. He became bandmaster of the Highland Light Infantry in 1898, and in 1903 was appointed to the Royal Garrison Artillery Band newly formed at Plymouth.

Mr. George McLaughlin, the bandmaster of the 2nd York and Lancaster Regiment, served in the R.A. Band, 1869-89.

Mr. Leonard Barker, late bandmaster of the Scots Greys (1882), and the 2nd Life Guards (1889), served in the R.A. Band, 1870-81.[1]

The following programmes are inserted as an illustration of the music performed by the R.A. Band at this period:—

ORCHESTRAL.

ROYAL ARTILLERY CONCERT,

Wednesday, 10th March, 1858.

PART I.

Symphony ... "Consecration of Sound" ... ... Spohr

Largo, Allegro, Tempo di Marcia, Andante Maestoso, Larghetto, Allegretto.

PART II.

Overture	...	"Siege of Rochelle"	...	...	Balfe
Selection No. 2	...	"Don Juan"	...	...	... Mozart
Chorus	...	"Song of the Miners"	...	Kücken
Duetto	...	...	"Nino"	...	...	... Nino
		Cornet, Trumpet-Major Lawson			
		Euphonium, Bombardier Lake			
Waltz ...	...	...	"Adelaide"	...	...	Lamotte

---

[1] At the present time there are two members of the R.A. Band at Kneller Hall training for bandmasters. These are Student F. W. Sylvester and Student R. E. Collier.

MILITARY BAND.

DEVON AND EXETER
BOTANICAL AND HORTICULTURAL SOCIETY,
Exeter, Thursday, July 22nd, 1858.

PART I.

Grand March	...	"Lucknow"	...	...	... Owen
Overture	...	"Das Nachtlager in Granada"	...		Kreutzer
Selection	...	... "Il Trovatore"	...	...	... Verdi
Quadrille	...	"Napoleon et Eugenie"			Dilara-Bright
Galop	...	... "Indian Dahk"	...	...	Smyth
Selection	...	"Lucia di Lammermoor"			Donizetti
Waltz	...	... "Adelaide"	...	...	Lamotte
Overture	...	... "Oberon"	...	...	... Weber

PART II.

March	...	... "The Princess Royal"	...	...	... Owen
Overture	...	... "I Martiri"	...	...	Donizetti
Waltz	...	... "Star of the West"	...		Montagne
Selection	...	... "The Rose of Castile"	...	...	... Balfe
Polka	...	... ...	...	...	... Jullien
Quadrille	...	... "The Bonnie Dundee"	...		D'Albert

Among other rules drawn up by the band committee in 1858 was one that "not less than thirty musicians to be permitted to go as the R.A. Band to any public entertainment," but this stringent rule could not have been rigorously enforced, for in the following year "eight musicians are allowed to go to a private party." Being known in every part of the country, Mr. Smyth soon obtained engagements for the band at Salisbury, Colchester, Bristol, High Elms, Birmingham, Exeter (which it visited in 1858-9-60-1-2-3-6 and 1868), York, Clifton, Oxford, Brighton, Liverpool, Hull, Gloucester, Coventry, Bishop's Auckland, Trowbridge, Tunbridge Wells, Ipswich, Devizes, Faversham, etc.

The success of the band on these occasions was such that the band committee desired to "congratulate the regiment on the high state of efficiency of the band"; and the orchestra especially had advanced to such a degree of excellence, that Mr. Smyth was constantly receiving most flattering letters from gentlemen of the highest musical standing. Sir Michael Costa was among the foremost of its patrons, and greatly interested himself in the band. He frequently engaged the principal performers in several of his orchestras.[1] So enthusiastic were the officers over the merits of the band, that in order that the musicians should get a thorough knowledge of the best music of the day, their expenses were paid to attend the opera, and also the concerts at Exeter Hall, and Ella's concerts. In 1861, fifty pounds was set apart for this purpose.

In 1859 the organisation of the regiment was changed from battalions, with stationery headquarters, to movable brigades, and it was thought that the R.A. Band would be broken up to furnish a band for each brigade, but nothing was done in this direction. Nearly all the brigades, however, formed bands on their own account, being trained by the brigade trumpet-majors,[2] who were nearly all appointed from the R.A. Band. The most important of these bands were those raised at the depôts—Warley and Sheerness.

The former was raised about 1861 from the band

[1] On these occasions Mr. Smyth would occupy the same desk as M. Sainton, the leader.
[2] Designated "Sergeant Trumpeters."—R.W., 1881.

of the Honourable East India Company, under the
direction of Mr. John Henrietta, and later Mr.
Duncan Moody, but was broken up in 1868.

The Sheerness band was formed about the same
time as the Warley Band, under the direction of
the trumpet-major. Mr. Charles McLaren[1] held
this position until the band was broken up in
1868, when he entered Kneller Hall as a student,
and became bandmaster of the 108th Regiment,
1870-90. He died at Secunderabad, 1898. About
1871 the Royal Artillery at Sheerness again raised
a band, under Sergeant Drecy, and afterwards
under Trumpet-Major Smith. In 1875, Mr. Charles
M. Glaysher, late of the R.A. Band, was appointed bandmaster, which position he held until
1883, and the band was disembodied soon afterwards.

Mr. Glaysher was born at Brentford in 1844,
and served in the R.A. Band, 1856-73. When only
twenty-one he was appointed organist at the
garrison church, St. George's, and had the honour
of being complimented by Charles Gounod. He
was also organist at St. Margaret's, Plumstead,
and at the Dockyard Church, Sheerness, 1879-1901.
He died in 1902.[2]

In 1862 the band of the Imperial Guards of
France and the Zouave Band, who were on a visit
to England, were entertained at Woolwich by the

[1] His brother John, who distinguished himself in the
Crimea, served in the R.A. Band.

[2] The late Mr. Charles Glaysher gave me the information
for this subject. His two sons are serving in the R.A. Band
at present.

R.A. Band, and on the eve of their departure, a farewell supper was given them in the regimental schools. Monsieur Reidel, *chef de musique*, of the Guards, presented the R.A. Band with an inscribed photograph of the Guards' band.[1]

On the 20th August, 1863, through the efforts of Mr. Smyth, the rank of honorary sergeant-major was granted to the band sergeant, and honorary quarter-master-sergeant to the next senior sergeant. Several deserving non-commissioned officers and men, the solo performers on each instrument, were given the rank of the honorary sergeant. The Christmas furlough was granted about the same time.

At the opening of St. George's (Garrison) Church, 2nd November, 1863, the R.A. Band, assisted by some ladies, and the band of the Royal Horse Artillery and the R.A. Bugle Band, in all about 250, sang " Lift up your heads " (Messiah) and Townshend Smith's anthem, " Oh, how amiable." The consecration ceremony was performed by the Bishop of London. Among those present were H.R.H. the Duke of Cambridge, Earl de Grey, Lord and Lady Sidney, the Quartermaster-General, Chaplain-General, and the *élite* of the neighbour-hood, who all expressed their gratification to Mr. Smyth.[2]

The first organists at this church were Madame Ernestine Smyth, the wife of the bandmaster, and Mr. Charles M. Glaysher, R.A.B., and for many

[1] Now in the R.A. Band Reading Room.

[2] *Musical World*, 7-11-1863.

years the choir was also furnished by the R.A. Band.

The old Artillery Chapel was now converted into a theatre (or, as it was called for a time, the Lecture Hall), and was formally opened with a grand concert, given by the band, on the 23rd December, 1863 :—

NEW LECTURE HALL, ROYAL ARTILLERY BARRACKS.

(Accommodation for One Thousand persons.)

By permission of Major-General Sir R. Dacres, K.C.B.,
Commandant of the Garrison.

A GRAND VOCAL AND INSTRUMENTAL CONCERT

BY THE CHORAL UNION, R.A.,

Consisting of upwards of 150 Voices ; and the

ORCHESTRAL BAND, R.A.,

Of Seventy Performers,

On WEDNESDAY, DECEMBER 23rd, 1863.

Solo Vocalists :
Misses CREELMAN, HUNTER and MAGRATH,
Messrs. MANSFIELD, MAYLOR and SMITH, R.A. Band.

PROGRAMME.

PART FIRST.

Overture	...	...	"Domino Noir"	Auber

Solo & Chorus "List to the gay castanet" (Rose of Castile) Balfe
Solo, Mr. Smith, R.A. Band

Air Stirien ... "Quick arise, Maiden Mine" ... Dessaur
Miss Creelman

Part Song ... ... "Hunting Song" ... Mendelssohn

Ballad ..."When other lips" (Bohemian Girl)... Balfe
Mr. J. Maylor, R.A. Band

Duet ... ... "May Bells" ... Mendelssohn
Misses Creelman and Hunter

Grand Selection ... Opera "Faust" ... ... Gounod
Introducing the celebrated chorus of soldiers, "Glory
and love to the men of old," for voices and orchestra,
Instrumental Solos by Messrs. Carpenter, Jullien
and Buckland, R.A. Band

PART SECOND

Overture ... ... "Guillaume Tell" ... ... Rossini

Ballad ... ... "The last good-bye" ... ... Wallace
Miss Magrath

Trio & Chorus "The Chough and Crow" ... Bishop

Solos, Misses Creelman, Hunter, and Mr. Smith, R.A. Band

Song "Yes! Let me like a soldier fall!" (Maritana) Wallace
Mr. A. Mansfield, R.A. Band

Solo for Cornet "Air and Variations" ... ... Levy
Mr. Carpenter, R.A. Band

Chorus ... ... "Here in cool grot" Lord Mornington

Quadrille on National Melodies, "The Lakes of Killarney"
Smyth

Solos for Cornet, Clarionet, Bassoon, and Piccolo, &c.,
Messrs. Carpenter, Julian, Montara and Browne,
R.A. Band

"God save the Queen."

CONDUCTOR, MR. J. SMYTH, R.A., BANDMASTER.

Prices of Admission for the General Public: Reserved
Numbered Stalls, 1/6; Gallery, Reserved Stalls, 1/-; Side
Boxes, 1/-; Pit, 6d. Admission for Military: Reserved
Numbered Stalls, 1/-; Gallery, Reserved Stalls, 6d.; Side
Boxes, 4d.; Pit, 3d. Children in arms not admitted.

The first theatrical performance in this theatre
was given on the 22nd February, 1864, by the
officers of the regiment and the Canterbury Old
Stagers. Among the latter were the present Sir
Spencer Ponsonby Fane, Sir Henry de Bathe, the
late Samuel Brandram, Earl Bessborough, and
other distinguished amateurs. Since then the
building has never been idle, for in addition to the
many performances given by both the officers and
men, an annual pantomime has been given since
1872. A portion of the R.A. Band has always
fulfilled the duties of the orchestra at this theatre,

under the direction of the sergeant-major, who invariably composed and arranged the music that was necessary.

On two occasions the late Frederick Clay produced operettas here, and Sir Francis Burnand also produced one of his inimitable burlesques, himself playing the principal character.

Many prominent actors and actresses have gained their earliest fame on these boards; among these may be mentioned Mr. H. B. Irving, Mr. Horace Mills, Miss Dorothea Baird, and the late Fred Leslie. The latter was the son of a sergeant in the Royal Artillery, and born at Artillery Place, Woolwich, in 1855. His immense success as a singer and actor is too well known to be repeated here. He used to relate that when he first applied for a professional engagement to Miss Kate Santley he told her, in reply to her enquiry, that he had had experience in the provinces, but if she had pressed him to produce notices, all he had were connected with the R.A. Theatre, Woolwich. He died in London in 1892, and was buried at Charlton Cemetery.

The Royal Artillery Concerts,[1] which were held in the Officers' Mess, were in 1864 transferred to the R.A. Theatre, and opened to the public. These concerts have always been held in the highest estimation by the inhabitants of Woolwich, for they at least maintain that "the R.A. Band is unsurpassed, not only in England, but probably

---

[1] A collection of R.A. concert programmes and others from 1846 to the present time is in the writer's possession.

throughout the world."[1] Royalty have frequently honoured these concerts by their presence, and notably the late Emperor Frederick of Germany, Empress Eugenie, Princess Frederica of Hanover (who attended twice), Prince George Galitzan,[2] Count Münster, and other distinguished persons.

" On the 25th November, 1868, the Prince and Princess Mary of Teck and the Princess Louise accompanied their Royal relative, Prince Arthur, to Woolwich, to attend the fourth of the series of afternoon concerts given . . . by the Royal Artillery Band, at which entertainments His Royal Highness has been a regular attendant . . . . . Though the intended visit was not announced until the morning of the day, there was an unusual demand for seats. The band was in full uniform.[3] The programme for the concert could not have been better chosen if the entertainment had been designed for the special occasion, though, except a waltz bespoken by Prince Arthur, there had been no idea of distinguishing this from any other of the series.

---

[1] *Warlike Woolwich.*—VINCENT.

[2] Here is a letter on the subject, addressed to Mr. Smyth :—

17, HANOVER SQUARE.
15th February, 1861.

SIR,—I have been so much surprised by the efficiency of the band under your direction, that I cannot refrain from expressing my satisfaction. I shall have great pleasure in letting you have some of the Russian music you desire, and would even not object to lead the band myself, if you thought my so doing would be agreeable to the society of Woolwich.
Yours truly,
PRINCE GEORGE GALITZAN.

[3] Full dress was only worn on special occasions. Undress uniform was worn at the R.A. concerts until December, 1874.

The symphony was Beethoven's *No. 2 in D*, a most beautiful work, to which it is needless to say that the utmost effect was given by this splendid corps of musicians . . . . This was followed by a selection from Auber's opera, *Le Premier Jour de Bonheur*, ... the first time of its performance, a production in which the Royal visitors manifested great pleasure . . . . of the oboe solo from *Don Pasquale*, played by Sergeant Jones, of the band, we cannot speak too highly; it was marvellously excellent, and was rewarded by the most sincere commendation, . . . the visitors were so delighted that they promised, if possible, to attend again at one or other of the two concerts which remain to complete the series."[1]

The programmes at these concerts, which were in many ways superior to those of Mr. Collins' *régime*, usually consisted of a symphony, an operatic selection (generally of Mr. Smyth's own admirable arrangement), two vocal pieces, an instrument solo (for both string and wind), which was a special feature in the band's performance, an overture, and one of Strauss' or Gung'l's waltzes.

The following is an extract from the *United Service Gazette*, January 8th, 1869 :—

" The series of winter concerts given by the band of the Royal Artillery were resumed at Woolwich on Wednesday, the 6th inst. We are not surprised at the esteem in which these concerts are held by the officers of the regiment and the gentry of the

[1] *Kentish Independent*, 28-11-68.

district. The music is of the best; it is rendered by a powerful band in a most artistic manner.

"The programme performed on Wednesday was the following:—Part I.—Symphony *No. 4*, Mozart. Part II.—Part. songs (1) *April Showers*, Hatton, (2) *Bring the Bowl*, F. Boot; overture, *Athalie*, Mendelssohn; flute solo, *Original Air with Variations*, Richardson (soloist, Sergeant J. A. Browne); operatic selection, *Il Trovatore*, Verdi; waltz, *Die Grafenberger*, Gung'l. The symphony was played with wonderful power and precision, and the efforts of the performers were warmly acknowledged; and as the other pieces were not less admirably played, the concert was in every respect most enjoyable. An interval was very agreeably occupied by the singing of Hatton's part song, *April Showers*, and a solo (Sergeant A. Mansfield) and chorus, *Bring the Bowl*, the whole strength of the band, upwards of sixty, taking part. The voices are admirably trained, and the effect was so marked as to make one astonished at the versatility of the performers, who play wind instruments and string, and sing equally well. . . . . The arrangement and execution of these concerts reflect the highest praise on Mr. Smyth, on whose exertions their success mainly depends."

In addition to those known as the R.A. Concerts, there were several series of high-class vocal and instrumental concerts given by the band, which were a great success. Madame Smyth, the wife of the bandmaster, a famous vocalist, organised a singing class, composed of young ladies in the town and garrison, many of them being daughters

of members of the band. These for a time sup-
planted the boys as sopranos in the band choir, or,
as it was now called, the R.A. Choral Union, which
sometimes numbered two hundred voices. They
performed choral works of every description—
operatic, oratorio, and even Mozart's *Twelfth Mass*
is found among their performances.

Several of these ladies afterwards became distinguished in the profession. We may name among
others, Miss Phillipine Siedle, Miss Julia Siedle
(now Madame Julia Lennox), and Miss Annie
Tremaine, known to a later generation as Madame
Amadi, of the Carl Rosa Opera. This lady was
known in Woolwich during the "sixties" as Miss
Creelman, then a pupil teacher at the regimental
schools (*see* programme on page 127). She was the
daughter of a sergeant in the Royal Artillery.

Signor Alberto Randegger conducted several
concerts in this theatre, assisted by several eminent
artistes, among whom were :—Madame Patey,
Madame Drasdil, Madame Rudersdorff, Madame
Emmeline Cole, Signor Pezze, Mr. W. H. Cum-
mings, and many others. Among the distinguished
amateurs who assisted may be mentioned the
present Lieut.-Col. Sir Arthur Bigge and the late
Colonel O. H. Goodenough, for whom Odoardi
Barri wrote his famous song, "The Old Brigade."

The officers and ladies of the garrison also gave
several series of concerts. They formed themselves
into an "Amateur Musical Society," and gave
frequent *soirées musicales*. Their programmes were
of considerable merit. On the following page is
one of them.

K

AMATEUR MUSICAL SOCIETY.

SOIRÉE MUSICALE, OCTOBER 19th, 1858.

PROGRAMME—PART I.

Overture	... ...	"Masaniello"	Auber
		Full Orchestra—Royal Artillery Band	
Part Song	... ...	"Ave Maria"	Smart
Trio ...	...	"Ti paego O Madre pia"	Curschmann
	Mrs. Franklin, Mrs. Leslie, and Lieut. Hicks, R.A.		
Aria ...	...	"Consider the lilies"	Topliff
		Mrs. Chataway	
Duetto	... "Quis est homo" (Stabat Mater) ...		Rossini
	Mrs. LeMesurier and Miss Larios		
Coro di Donne	... "Robert le Diable "	...	Meyerbeer
Song ...	... ...	"L'Espagnole" ...	... ...
		Miss Larios	

Concerted Instrumental Pot-pourri, arranged for
the occasion from "Robert le Diable " ...   } Meyerbeer
Pianoforte, Mrs. Freeth and Miss Gore ; flute, Major
Gore ; cornet, Major Simpson, R.A. ; clarionet,
Captain Clerk, R.A. ; Stringed Quintett, Mr. Smyth
and members of the R.A. Band

PART II.

Overture	... ...	..." Martha "	Flotow
		Royal Artillery Band	
Part Song	...	... "The Departure" ...	Mendelssohn
Duet ...	... ...	"O lovely peace"	Haydn
	Mrs. Freeth and Mrs. Chataway		
Cavatina	"Reguava nel Silenzio " (Lucia di. L.)		Donizetti
	Mrs. LeMesurier		
Trio ...	...	"L'usato Ardir " (Semiramide) ...	Rossini
	Mrs. Farmer, Mrs. Leslie and Mr. Hillier		
Solo, Pianoforte	...	"Cracovienne"	Wallace
		Mrs. Dames	
Trio ...	... ...	"L'Espagnole "	Pinsuti
	Mrs. Freeth, Mrs. LeMesurier and Miss Larios		
Chorus	... ...	"Bohemian Girl "	Balfe

"God save the Queen" as Solo, Quartett and Chorus
Mrs. Franklin, Miss Mitchell, Captain Carpenter, R.A.,
and Major Simpson, R.A., with Chorus

The last concerts we shall mention in connection
with the R.A. Theatre are the musical "At Homes,"
given by the present Lieut.-Colonel H. W. L. Hime,
R.A., from 1881 to 1885. This officer, a highly
cultured musician and a pianist of considerable
ability, will be remembered in musical circles as
the author of "Wagnerism," a protest against
Wagnerian music. The programmes at his "At

Homes" were of the highest order, containing some of the rarely-heard chamber music of the great masters, several of which were presented for the first time in England; and one, Spohr's *Trio in D flat*, had never before been heard in public. It was through his efforts that Haydn's *Passione* was performed by the R.A. Band at St. George's Church, for the first time probably since the composer's death.

A programme of one of these "At Homes," is appended:—

26th JANUARY, 1882.—PART I.

1. Largo, Op. 1., No. 2 ... ... Beethoven

Violin ... Bombardier E. Beech, R.A. Band
'Cello ... „ G. Shearer, „
Piano ... Major Hime, R.A.

2. Notturno ... ... Spohr
Movements : *Marcia, Polacca, Adagio, Allegro*

Flute ... Sergeant F. Harris
Violin ... Bombardier E. Beech
Viola ... Musician W. Cooke } R.A. Band
Cello ... Bombardier G. Shearer
Piano ... Musician W. Guest

3. Mass in F ... { "Benedictus"
"Agnus Dei" } ... Schubert
"Dona Nobis Pacem" }

Treble ... Master F. Jones
Alto ... „ C. Barton
1st Tenor Mr. Theodore Barth
2nd Tenor Musician T. Burt, R.A. Band
Bass ... „ H. Smith, „

PART II.

4. Adagio, Op. 30, No 2 ... ... Beethoven

Violin ... Bombardier E. Beech, R.A. Band
Piano ... Major Hime, R.A.

5. Quartett ... ... Weber
Movements : *Allegro, Adagio, Presto*

Piano ... Miss Lovey
Violin ... Bombardier E. Beech
Viola ... Musician W. Cooke } R.A. Band
'Cello ... Bombardier G. Shearer

6. The Requiem { "Recordare"
"Lachrymosa"
"Agnus Dei" } ... ... Mozart
"Sanctus" }

K 2

There are several ladies and gentlemen connected with the Royal Artillery who have risen to the highest honours in the musical world. Miss Beatrice Langley,[1] one of the best living English violinists, is the daughter of Colonel W. S. Langley, R.A. Willett Adye, an amateur violinist of considerable reputation, and author of *Musical Notes* (London, 1869), was the son of Major J. Pattison Adye, R.A.

Charles Manners, the celebrated bass singer, who is making such a noble effort to establish a national English opera, is Southcote Mansergh, fourth son of Paymaster-Colonel J. C. Mansergh, late R.H.A. Herbert Thorndike, a well-known baritone vocalist, is the son of the Rev. C. F. Thorndike, late R.A., and grandson of the late General Daniel Thorndike, R.A. Gilberto Ghilberti, a bass vocalist who sings in opera, oratorio and concerts, is in reality Gilbert J. Campbell, son of Major-General T. Hay Campbell, Royal (Madras) Artillery.

One of the few ladies who have achieved success as a composer of classical music is Miss Ethel Smyth, the daughter of General J. H. Smyth, R.A.[2]

A famous opera singer, known to the wide world as Margaret Macintyre, is the daughter of General J. Mackenzie Macintyre, Royal (Madras) Artillery.

[1] This lady has played at the R.A. Concerts, as also another well-known violinist, Louis Pecskai, his first appearance in this country.

[2] It is said her talents were first seriously noticed by Lieutenant-Colonel Ewing, the composer of "Jerusalem the Golden," who persuaded her parents to send her to Leipsic to complete her musical education.

The last we shall mention is a composer known as
"Dolores," whose songs acquired a considerable
amount of popularity in their day. "Dolores" was
the *nom-de-plume* of Ellen Dickson, daughter of
Sir Alexander Dickson, R.A.

The principal instrumental performers in the R.A.
Band in 1864 were :—

Flute, Sergeant J. A. Browne[1]; oboe, Corporal G.
Jones ; B flat clarionet, Sergeant-Major J. Farlie[2];
B flat clarionet, Sergeant F. Julian[3]; bassoon,
Sergeant J. Montara[4]; cornet, Corporal J. Car-
penter[5]; horn, Corporal C. Buckland[6]; althorn,
Sergeant G. C. Smith; trombone, Musician J.
Hunt[7]; euphonium, Sergeant G. Buckland; violin
(leader), Sergeant-Major J. Farlie; viola, Sergeant
J. Smith[8]; violoncello, Sergeant J. Clementi.[9]

The names of some of these performers occur in

---

[1] Became bandmaster, Royal Horse Artillery (*see*
Chap. VII.).

[2] Became bandmaster of militia.

[3] One of the finest players of his day. Another member
of the band, B. C. Bent, became one of the finest cornet
players in America, and was for some time with Gilmore.

[4] A very fine performer. For many years in the
Alhambra orchestra, died 1890. He was educated at the
Brussels Conservatoire. His son became sergeant-major
of the band.

[5] An excellent performer. Pupil of the late J. Lawson.
Died 1867.

[6] Afterwards solo cornet. Became bandmaster of the
Norfolk Artillery.

[7] Became bandmaster of volunteers at Maidstone.

[8] He was quartermaster-sergeant of the band and
principal bass vocalist for many years; now residing at
Amersham. I am indebted to him for much information.

[9] Grand nephew of the famous pianist, Muzio Clementi.

a poem that appeared in the *Kentish Independent* in 1864[1] :—

" Hark ! borne on the wings of the soft summer breeze,
  That like sweet fairy kisses, stir softly the trees,
  Comes a full wave of melody, thrilling and glad,
  Such as never the wild harp of Orpheus had ;
  And you can't help but stay on your journey to hear
  The sweet sound as it rises so lovingly near,
  Till your soul feels a witchery, solemn and grand,
  Woke to life by the noble Artillery Band."

" See under the trees where, like beautiful blooms,
  Fair woman with brightness the shadow illumes,
  There Woolwich pours out in its beauty and pride
  When the sun lights the hills from the western side ;
  There Smyth waves his bâton, as magi of old
  Would, when charming base metal to silver and gold,
  Till so gently, well up, 'neath his masterly hand,
  Floods of melody from the Artillery Band."

" Hear Carpenter's cornet burst out with a sound,
  Making silvery all the full echoes around,
  Or Gritton or Chapman repeat the full strain
  Till the very hills tremble with gladness again ;
  Or Buckland's loud horn, like the thunder of war,
  Bid the heroes around think of past fields afar,
  With him Naylor the singer, and young Gordon stand
  In thy ranks, O soul-winning Artillery Band."

" Hear Pattison's bass like the thunder of Jove,
  With him bright Barney Keard, rather given to rove,
  Or Montara's bassoon that trembles the air,
  Or Browne's soft, sweet flute pours its melody rare ;
  There's Julian's clarionette, the oboe of Jones,
  Swell out with famed Farlie the overture's tones,
  Oh, say, thou goddess of music, what land
  Hath such minstrels as thine own Artillery Band."

[1] Written by " C. J.," Rectory Grove, Woolwich.

" And many there are, too, full worthy of fame
  That to me are unknown, but the grand deathless
    name
  That has wreathed them for years, shall for ever
    remain.
  E'en though Godfrey's Guards try their laurels to gain,
  E'en though France sends her Guides, and proud
    Austria boast
  Of the bandsmen that lead on her white-crested host,
  Their fame is but footprints along the ocean's sand,
  But the proud rocks are thine, O Artillery Band."

" When in peace through the town, o'er the heath,
    through the lanes,
  Come the echoing sounds of thy silvery strains ;
  Sturdy labour and age, maid and matron and child,
  Throng, out of their cares for a moment beguiled.
  But when war calls the soldier to battle and death,
  Then like fire to his heart comes thy soul-stirring
    breath,
  And he cheers as the ship leaves his dear native land
  To thy grand thrilling music, Artillery Band."

During the visit of the French fleet to Portsmouth
in April, 1866, the R.A. Band was in attendance
with Jullien's celebrated band.

On the occasion of the state entry of the Duke
and Duchess of Edinburgh into London, the R.A.
Band, with the R.H.A. Band and the R.A. Brass
Band, took part in the ceremony, March, 1874.

The band attended the funeral of H.R.H. the
Prince Imperial of France, 1879.

Towards the close of 1879,[1] the Duke of Cam-

[1] About this time a library and reading-room was opened
for the band, and several of the officers made presents of
books and assisted in furnishing the room, notably Colonel
Goodenough and Major Hime. The library contains some
eighty volumes of text-books, tutors, vocal scores and
libretti of operas, oratorios, and other works.

bridge, approved of a new undress uniform for the band, a patrol being introduced instead of the shell jacket. It was taken into wear in 1880, and is worn at the present time. It consists of a dark blue patrol with scarlet collar, the front edges, collar and cuffs being laced with gold tracing lace; gold cord shoulder straps, and gilt grenades for the collar. The sergeant-major and quartermaster-sergeant wear a similar patrol, with some additional lacing.

In the summer of 1880 Mr. Smyth was granted leave of absence, pending retirement, and during the spring of 1881 he retired to Forest Hill, and for a few years regularly attended the musical festivals at the Crystal Palace, where Mr. (now Sir August) Manns frequently played his selections.

He could not be called a great musician, but he was pre-eminently fitted for his position. He had a thorough knowledge of every instrument in the band, even in his advanced years studying the harp. His judgment was at all times sound; he was known and respected by Balfe, Costa, Jullien, Manns, and other leading conductors.[1] In 1860 he was one of the judges at the Crystal Palace Brass Band Contest, the first contest held in the south of England.[2] He was also one of a jury, with Sir Arthur Sullivan, Sir Jules Benedict, Signor Arditi, and others engaged by the Alhambra Company to adjudicate at a musical composition contest in 1871.

[1] *British Musician*, Sept., 1898.
[2] *Music for the People.*—MARR, 1889.

SERGEANT-MAJOR,
ROYAL ARTILLERY BAND,
1879.

enades for
rtermaster
additio... i

but he
He had
in the

...d ...
adjudic.
...1.

SERGEANT-MAJOR,
ROYAL ARTILLERY BAND,
1879.

Although his own compositions were in no way remarkable (being mostly marches, dance music, etc.), yet his arrangements for orchestra and military band were highly commended by some of the leading men of his time. On the 3rd August, 1865, Sir Michael Costa dined with the R.A. officers at Woolwich, when the band played—overture, *William Tell*, Rossini; selection, *L'Africaine*, Meyerbeer; march, *Eli*, Costa; selection, *Dinorah*, Meyerbeer; and the scherzo from Beethoven's symphony *No. 8*. He expressed himself very much delighted with the performance, but was puzzled over the selection *L'Africaine*, and he asked Mr. Smyth where he obtained it, as it was instrumented exactly as Meyerbeer did himself, and he knew there were only two full scores in existence, and it had only been produced in London a few days before.[1] So impressed was Sir Michael that he presented him with his oratorio, *Naaman*, and asked him to make a selection from it. The following is a letter on the subject :—

"59, ECCLESTON SQUARE,
"September 25th, 1865.

"DEAR SIR,—I have had the pleasure to send you by rail the full score of my oratorio 'Naaman,' as I promised, and hope that you will arrange some of the pieces for your splendid military band, which gave me much gratification for all that they played under your able direction, also as an 'Orchestre Band,' and I was agreeably surprised at their singing glees so well.

[1] The fact was Smyth had heard the opera in Paris, and having the vocal and piano score with him, he made notes of the most striking or peculiar instrumentation as he heard it.

"I have no doubt that the officers of the
regiment must feel very much satisfaction in
having a gentleman of your talent to preside
over such a distinguished body of Musicians.
Trusting that you may long be spared for the
good of Art,

"Believe me, yours very truly,

"M. Costa."

Sir Michael attended one of the R.A. Concerts
in February, 1869, when the selection from *Naaman*
was performed, and expressed his appreciation. He
also came to Woolwich the following year specially
to hear the band (military) play in the Repository.

Sir Jules Benedict also wished Mr. Smyth to
arrange the "Wedding March," to be sent to
Russia, on the occasion of the marriage of the
Duke of Edinburgh.

Under Mr. Smyth the band performed in all parts
of the country.[1] The French Government applied
for the band to visit Paris, and Lord Granville told
Mr. Smyth that application was made for it to
visit Boston, U.S.A., to take part in the peace cele-
brations in 1872, but the Grenadier Guards Band
was sent instead, as it was thought that the British
Army would be better represented by red coats.
Applications have since been made for the band to
visit Hamburg, Berlin, Cape Colony and Canada.

Early in 1885 Mr. Smyth took ill, and died on
7th September following; he was buried at Charlton
Cemetery, not many yards from Woolwich Com-

[1] In 1864, Mr. Smyth was presented with a handsome
bâton from the officers of the R.A. and R.E. at Portsmouth,
and the following year they presented him with a valuable
silver cup, much prized by him.

mon, where his reputation had been chiefly made.

The principal instrumental performers during the later years of Mr. Smyth's *régime* were :—

Flute, Sergeant F. Harris; oboe, Sergeant G. Browne[1]; E flat clarionet, Sergeant W. Williams; B flat clarionet, Sergeant E. Burt; bassoon, Sergeant J. C. Montara[2]; cornet, Quartermaster-Sergeant C. Buckland[3]; horn, Bombardier J. Wilkinson; trombone, Sergeant W. J. Watts; euphonium, Sergeant J. Findlay; violin (leader), Sergeant W. Wells; viola, Corporal T. Cuthbertson; 'cello, Sergeant J. Findlay.

Mr. Albert Mansfield, the sergeant-major, was, on Mr. Smyth's retirement, appointed acting bandmaster, a position he held with great credit to himself and honour to his corps for fifteen months. He was born at Fareham, Hampshire, about 1842, and at a local concert his singing was noticed by Sir Fenwick Williams, the Commandant of Woolwich, who was on a visit to that town, and finding the boy willing, he enlisted him to join the R.A. Band. When his voice broke, it developed into a powerful tenor, and for many years, as the principal tenor vocalist, he sang at concerts in all parts of the country. He also became one of the leading violinists in the orchestra, and first clarionet in the military band.

In 1870 he was appointed sergeant-major, and he also became bandmaster of the Royal Caledonian

---

[1] Now in the Palace Theatre orchestra.
[2] Became bandmaster of Militia Artillery at Scarborough.
[3] Became bandmaster of the Norfolk Artillery.

Asylum. When Mr. Smyth went on leave pending discharge,[1] Mr. Mansfield took his position until a bandmaster was appointed, although it was almost settled that he should succeed to the position. He had given every satisfaction, and was favoured by the officers. In 1881 he successfully organised and conducted two concerts given at St. James' Hall, in aid of the service charities, etc., which were highly commented upon by those in a position to sanction his appointment as bandmaster; and on the 15th July of the same year the band was commanded to play at Windsor Castle, where it performed (military) in the quadrangle, and the late Queen Victoria personally complimented Mr. Mansfield, expressing her approbation of the performance of the band.

The programme performed on this occasion was:—

1. March	...	...	"Rienzi"	...	...	Wagner
2. Overture	...	...	"Oberon"	...	...	Weber
3. Reminiscences of Verdi	...	...	...	...		Smyth
4. Ungarische Tanze	...	...	...	...	...	Brahms
5. Waltz	...	...	"Chantilly"	...	...	Waldteufel
6. Reminiscences of Mozart	...	...	...		...	Mansfield
7. Dance Bohemian	...	"Les Fauvettes"	...		...	Bosquet
8. Selection	...	"Pirates of Penzance"		...	Sullivan
9. Russian Dance	...	...	...	...	...	Glinka
10. Caprice Militaire	...	...	...	...	...	Herzeele
11. Ave Maria	...	...	...	...	...	Schubert
12. Galop	...	...	...	"Victoria"		De Lara Bright
13. Part Song	"O, who will o'er the Downs"		...	Pearsall
14. Part Song	...	"Night, Lovely Night"		...	Berger

There was, however, a division among the officers concerning the appointment of a new bandmaster;

---

[1] When Mr. Smyth retired he was presented with a large photograph of the whole of the band, inscribed:— "A souvenir of affection and esteem from the members of the R.A. Band to Mr. Smyth, R.A. Bandmaster, 1881." It is now in the possession of W. F. Howe, Esq., Brighton.

one party advocated a selection by the band
committee, and the other insisted on an open
competitive examination under a committee of
professional musicians totally unconnected with
the regiment. The latter scheme was adopted,
and a special sub-committee of officers was formed,
consisting of Lieutenant-Colonel (afterwards Sir
Charles) Nairne, Major H. W. L. Hime, Captain
E. C. Trollope, Mus. Bac.,[1] and two others, who
were to receive the applications for the appointment. There were forty-four applicants, including
several gentlemen of high musical standing. Four
of these[2] were selected for the examination, which
was held at Kneller Hall, under the present Sir
August Manns.[3]

The successful candidate for bandmaster, R.A.,
was Cavaliere Ladislao Zavertal, an eminent conductor, resident at Glasgow.

[1] Another officer of the regiment who has taken a
musical degree is Colonel Chamier, R.H.A., Mus. Bac.

[2] Mr. Mansfield was one of them, but his health had for
some time been uncertain, and he failed to satisfy the
appointed examiners at Kneller Hall. He continued to act
as sergeant-major of the band, during which time the
officers tried to secure for him a commission as quarter-
master, but the authorities were afraid to set a precedent,
and another disappointment followed. He took his discharge in 1882, and in March, 1885, he became bandmaster
of the Queen's Westminster Volunteers, a position he held
until 1899, when he retired under the age clause. So highly
esteemed was Mr. Mansfield that a farewell benefit concert
was given him at Queen's Hall, Buckingham Gate, under
the patronage of the Duke and Duchess of Westminster,
Colonel Sir Howard Vincent, and the officers of the corps.
He died in October, 1900.

[3] The officers of the regiment presented Mr. Manns
with a valuable bâton in recognition of his services, which
was handed to him by the late Sir Charles Nairne. This
officer took a great interest in the band, and was among
the foremost of its patrons.

Photo by Elliott & Fry, Baker Street.

Ladislao Zavertal, M.V.O.

Photo by Elliott & Fry, Baker Street.

CHAPTER VI.

1881-1904.

"By'r lady, he is a good musician."
—"KING HENRY IV."

"And gazing on his fervent hands that made
The might of music, all their souls obeyed
With trembling strong subservience of delight."
—SWINBURNE.

CAVALIERE LADISLAO JOSEPH
PHILLIP PAUL ZAVERTAL was
born at Milan, on the 29th September,
1849, in one of the houses now forming part of
the Hôtel Manin, which at that time belonged to
his mother's family. It was in this house that
Mozart's son, Carlo, breathed his last, tended
until the end by Venceslao H. Zavertal and
Carlotta Maironi, nobile da Ponte, the father and
mother of Cavaliere Zavertal,[1] both of whom were
musicians of considerable repute.

Cavaliere Zavertal was the second son, and after
having been taught the violin and pianoforte at

---

[1] From Carlo Mozart the late Mr. V. H. Zavertal
received several precious autographs of his (Mozart's)
illustrious father, including a letter written after the first
performance of *Il Flauto Magico*, also an oil painting of the
great Mozart's wife, Constanze Weber. These interesting
treasures are now in Cavaliere Zavertal's possession.

home, for his parents were his first teachers,[1] he was sent to pursue his studies at the Conservatoire at Naples, where he took a scholarship for violin playing. Here Tosti was his *maëstrino*, or pupil teacher, for the violin. But as his *métier* was composition, he did not remain there for any length of time.

He made his first appearance as a composer in his fifteenth year at Milan, and the following year published some pianoforte music. When only nineteen, he wrote in collaboration with his father, then the Director of the Municipal School of Music at Treviso, an opera in three acts, entitled *Tita*, which had a marked success, but it could not hold its place in the *répertoires* on account of the libretto, which was weak and written in dialect. It is interesting to note that Gayarre, the celebrated tenor, who learnt the score in three days to the amazement of the composers, virtually began his career with this opera.

Mr. Zavertal next returned to Milan, and at the age of twenty entered the orchestra of a Milanese theatre, and two months later he was appointed conductor and composer to the same theatre. In this capacity he wrote several successful operettas, and made a name for himself as an orchestral

---

[1] His father was a conductor and composer of great ability, on whom the Italian Government conferred the *Cittadinanza Italiana*. He saw much service in the wars of 1859-60, being present at the siege of Ancona, and received honourable mention of his bravery from King Victor Emanuel II. For many years he was Director of the Conservatoires of Treviso and Modena. He came to England in 1874, and resided at Helensburgh, near Glasgow, where he was highly esteemed as a conductor and teacher.

conductor, receiving favourable notice from many eminent critics, including the well-known " Fillippo Fillippi " of the *Perseveranza*. At one of these operettas, *Sura Palmira Sposa*, Princess Margherite of Savoy, now Dowager Queen of Italy, was present.

In 1871, just after the Franco-German War, he came to Glasgow, where the conductorship of two musical societies had been offered him. Here he came in contact with Dr. Hans Von Bülow, whose orchestra he conducted for a time, accompanying him on a concert tour to Edinburgh, Dundee, and other towns in Scotland. He relates how he was visited at a late hour one night by an emissary of the Choral Union, and asked if he would undertake the duties of conductor, someone being wanted immediately to fill the position. It was short notice, for he had both rehearsal and concert on the following day, and the work was unknown to him, but all went well, and Von Bülow expressed on this as on many other occasions his appreciation of the abilities of Cavaliere Zavertal.[1]

He also conducted the Glasgow Orchestral Society, Hillhead Musical Association (which he held for ten years), and the Pollokshields Musical Association,[2] which he took over from his father, then in failing health.

Towards the close of 1881, the bandmastership of the Royal Artillery fell vacant, owing to the retirement of Mr. Smyth, and Cavaliere Zavertal was the successful candidate for the position. He

[1] *Strand Musical Magazine*, Aug., 1897.
[2] *Music and Musicians.*—MARR, 1887.

was appointed on the 10th December, 1881, but did not take his duties over until the New Year. He was the first bandmaster of the Royal Artillery to receive the warrant rank; his predecessors were generally staff-sergeants. Under Cavaliere Zavertal's fostering care the R.A. Band has attained a degree of excellence never before reached by an army band, and has consequently fulfilled many important engagements, both as an orchestra and a military band.

The band was engaged at the International Health Exhibition, 1884—at the opening ceremony, 8th May, and during August and October. In 1885 it was present at the opening of the Alexandra Palace Exhibition, and at the opening of the International Inventions Exhibition, 4th May, 1885, and played there during August, October, November, and at the closing ceremony.

In July, 1886, H.M. King Edward VII. (then Prince of Wales) selected the R.A. Band to play at Marlborough House State Ball. It was also engaged the same year at the International Exhibition, Edinburgh, and at the National Art Exhibition, Folkestone.

Her (late) Majesty Queen Victoria graciously commanded the band (orchestral) to play at Windsor Castle during the State Dinner, on the occasion of the visit of the Emperor and Empress of Germany, 25th June, 1887, when the Queen twice expressed her very great pleasure to Cavaliere Zavertal, and Her Majesty remained in the room until the end of the programme, which was very unusual for her to do. The band also took part in the Jubilee celebration, being stationed at Buckingham Palace. In this year it was engaged at the Royal Jubilee Exhibition, Manchester.

On the 26th August, 1887, the R.A. Mounted Band at Woolwich was finally disembodied, twelve of its members being drafted into the R.A. Band, which was now ordered to provide a mounted portion from its own ranks, to consist of :—

1 Sergeant (in charge)
2 Acting Bombardiers
17 Bandsmen
—
20

It was headed by a pair of silver kettledrums, without bannerols, carried by a grey horse.

On the 9th August, 1897, the dissolution of the mounted portion was ordered, the members taking their usual places in the R.A. Band.

During 1888 the band performed from May to November, including the closing ceremony, at the Colonial and Indian Exhibition. It was also engaged at the International Exhibition, Glasgow, from the opening ceremony, 8th May, to 21st May, and from 29th October to the closing ceremony. Cavaliere Zavertal, at the composer's request, scored for the military band Dr. Mackenzie's *Inaugural Ode*, written for and performed at the opening of the exhibition. He also acted as the adjudicator at the military band contests held in connection with the exhibition. The band was also engaged at the Anglo-Danish Exhibition, and the Fisheries Exhibition, 1888, and at the Spanish Exhibition the following year.

In May, 1889, a series of orchestral concerts
were inaugurated, at Cavaliere Zavertal's suggestion, at St. James' Hall, Piccadilly, four to be given
annually.[1] These invitation concerts have proved
immensely popular, and receive high praise from
the London Press. Commenting on the first
concert (8th May), the *British Bandsman* says :—
" The concert was quite a startling feature, as no
outsider suspected any British Army corps capable
of bringing to the front an excellent orchestra
which can with ease compete with the best existing.
Excepting the Philharmonic, the Richter, and Mr.
Manns' orchestras, which are generally formed of
the pick of the profession, we do not know in
London an orchestra which can equal the Royal
Artillery Band. Conductors wishing to learn how
lights and shades are to be thrown into an orchestral performance might study Mr. Zavertal's
conductorship—their time will not be wasted. The
performance of the overture *Mignon*, and of Liszt's
Hungarian rhapsody *No. 1*, were great features of
bravura, and took the audience by surprise. The
reading, particularly of the rhapsody, challenges
comparison with Richter's performance of the same
piece, although in that case Mr. Zavertal's merit
is far greater, as in his band he has certainly
not such qualified musicians as the Viennese conductor."

The following is an extract from a pamphlet
published by the officers, R.A., concerning these
concerts :—" Nothing, however, has tended to

[1] Only two concerts were given in the first year.

increase the reputation of the band as these public exhibitions of its capabilities before crowded London audiences. Letters of congratulation and appreciation are constantly received by the Secretary from those who are evidently lovers of music and critics of the art in its highest sense; and it was recently represented to the Committee that the band should no longer hide its light under a private bushel, but should court public criticism and invite professional attention to its performances, with a view to ascertaining whether, as was supposed, it could compete with other and better-known string bands, and justly claim a place amongst the orchestras of the kingdom."[1]

The *Daily Telegraph*,[2] 21st November, 1892, says:—"From an executive point of view their character is high, while it is the care of Cavaliere Zavertal, the conductor, to make the programmes worthy of an audience.[3] In a very distinct sense, therefore, the band of the Royal Regiment is one of the musical institutions of the metropolis. If anyone present went to St. James' Hall[4] with an

[1] "Herr Strauss is a great conductor of dance music, and his orchestra thoroughly understands him, but in other respects our colours need not be lowered, for have we not our unequalled Royal Artillery String Band?"—*Musical Standard*.

[2] The *Daily Telegraph* ranked the R.A. Band with the King of Würtemberg's Band, which took first prize at the Paris Exhibition.

[3] Sir Arthur Sullivan, speaking to Cavaliere Zavertal on one occasion at Ascot (an engagement the band has fulfilled for twenty years), said: "You are playing music, it is a pleasure to listen to you."

[4] These concerts were transferred to Queen's Hall, Langham Place, in 1894, where they are still held.

idea that allowance would have to be made for military musicians, he must have been pleasantly surprised. The Royal Artillery orchestra has a right to be heard anywhere and to play anything on precisely the same conditions as any other band. It is qualified to take rank among the best, and entitled to be judged by the highest standard."

The *Musical Times*, 1st December, 1892, says :— " The performances on this occasion reached a higher level than before, a fact which seems to indicate that further advance towards the ever-receding goal of perfection may be confidently expected. To descend to particulars—the playing showed an attention to detail and an amount of care and finish that might very well be regarded as a model for other musical organisations."

The *Sunday Times*, 20th November, 1892, says :— " The Royal Artillery has reason to be proud of its band. We wonder how many regiments in the world can muster such a capable and well-trained body of orchestral players. . . . In many respects the performance of these things could not have been improved upon."

At these concerts H.R.H. Princess Christian, the late Duke of Cambridge, Earl Roberts, and most of the artillery officers, past and present, have been regular attendants. The following letter from H.R.H. the Duke of Cambridge, then Commander-in-Chief, addressed to the General Officer Commanding at Woolwich, was published. This official congratulation to the officers and band alike was an honour never before bestowed on a military band in our service.

"Horse Guards,
"29th April, 1895.

Sir,—I have the command of His Royal Highness the Commander-in-Chief to inform you that His Royal Highness was present at the concert given by the Royal Regiment of Artillery on the 26th April, at the Queen's Hall, and was much pleased with the excellent taste displayed in the selection of the programme, and still more with the magnificent execution of the various pieces.

"His Royal Highness is satisfied that the high merit attained by the band of the Royal Artillery is due alike to the interest taken in it by the regiment at large and the talents and energy possessed by Cavaliere Zavertal and the members of the band.

"His Royal Highness commands me to express his great pleasure in having been present on this occasion, and desires that you will be good enough to convey this expression of approval to the President of the Band Committee and to Cavaliere Zavertal.

"I am, etc.,
"(Signed) F. T. Lloyd, d.a.o."

The programme played on the occasion referred to was[1] :—

PART I.

1. Symphony ... "Lenore" (No. 5) ... ... Raff
Allegro, Andante Quasi Larghetto, Tempo di Marcia, Agitato, Allegro

---

[1] The *Times*, commenting on the concert, said :—

". . . . The concert given . . . . in the Queen's Hall by the splendid band of the Royal Artillery was in every way as enjoyable as its predecessors. A remarkably fine performance of Raff's gruesome, but extraordinary clever *Lenore* symphony occupied the first part of the concert, the horn passages in the vigorous march being played with rare beauty of tone and precision. . . *Abendruhe*, by Loeschhorn, for strings only, one of Liszt's Hungarian rhapsodies, and Grieg's *Solvejg Lied*, were all beautifully played with the delicacy or force as occasion required, which have raised the band to its high estate."

PART II.

2. From the incidental music to "Cleopatra"...   Mancinelli
    (a.) "Triumphal March"
    (b.) "Andante" (Barcarolle)
    (c.) "Overture"

3.   ...   ...   "Abendruhe" (for strings)...   Loeschhorn

4.   ...   "Ungarische Rhapsodie," No. 2 in D   ...   Liszt

5.   ...   .   "Solveig's Lied"   ...   ...   Grieg
    (From Peer Gynt Suite, No. 2)

6. Overture ...   ...   "Tannhäuser" ...   .   Wagner

The principal instrumental performers in 1890 were:—

Flute, Bombardier D. Green; oboe, Bombardier W. Hayward[1]; B flat clarionet, Musician W. Johnstone; B flat clarionet, Sergeant W. Foster; bassoon, Quartermaster-Sergeant W. Houston[2]; cornet, Sergeant S. Jenner[3]; horn, Corporal W. Sugg[4]; althorn, Corporal W. Robinson[5]; trombone, Bombardier E. Parnum[6]; euphonium, Bombardier H. Gepp; harp, Bombardier D. Green[7]; violin (leader), Bombardier A. Cunningham[8]; viola, Musician L. Myers[9]; 'cello, Sergeant-Major E. Walker.[10]

Her late Majesty Queen Victoria graciously commanded the band (orchestral) to play during dinner at Windsor Castle, 21st November, 1890, and again

---

[1] Now in the Alhambra orchestra and oboe professor at Kneller Hall.
[2] Now in the orchestra at the Borough Theatre, Stratford.
[3] Became bandmaster, 3rd Lanark Rifle Volunteers, now in the orchestra at the London Hippodrome.
[4] Now musical director, Grand Theatre, Woolwich.
[5] At present in Dan Godfrey's orchestra at Bournemouth.
[6] Now in the orchestra at the Borough Theatre, Stratford.
[7] Now in the orchestra at the Empire Theatre.
[8] Now bandmaster, R.A. Band, Dover.
[9] Now musical director, Empire, Leeds.
[10] Now bandmaster, Honourable Artillery Company.

on the 7th July, 1891, and also at a similar function
at Buckingham Palace, 5th July, 1893.

In May, 1895, the band was engaged (orchestral)
at the Sunday Concerts at the Royal Albert Hall,
South Kensington, an engagement it still fulfils,
drawing immense audiences. On the occasion of a
Special Memorial Concert, after the death of the
late Queen, some hundreds were turned away from
the doors unable to gain admittance, and the
concert had to be repeated on the following Sunday.
Another record audience was at the Coronation
Sunday Concert, when some twelve thousand
people were present.

The *Metronome*, a New York paper, says :—

" The customary interregnum has been observed
at the Sunday afternoon concerts at the Royal
Albert Hall, Cavaliere Zavertal and his splendid
Royal Artillery Orchestra[1] of eighty, having taken
their usual holiday after playing one of the best
season's round concerts in this magnificent hall
they have ever played. The idle twaddle which
was talked a year or two ago about the coming
disbandment of this fine body of players has long
since passed out of notice, and the band, either as
military band or an orchestra, is to-day as fine as
ever; while in the matter of *répertoire* it is positively
unique. To hear them thunder out the *Kaisermarsch*
of Wagner, and then murmur the *La Colombe*
entr'acte of Gounod, is something to go home and
think about for days. Dynamic force or dove-like
tenderness is all the same to these splendidly

---

[1] It now attends every fourth Sunday as a military band.

trained musicians and their keenly intelligent chief, who is *au fait* with every class of music."

The *Daily Telegraph* says :—

" It is agreeable to learn that very soon Cavaliere Zavertal, a musician to the tips of his fingers, will once again be at hand with the string band of the Royal Artillery to make pleasant music for the *habitués* of these concerts. . . . . Their playing gains in finish and *feu sacré* year by year, and it is a joy to listen to them."

On the 12th June, 1895, a grand military concert was given at the Queen's Hall, Langham Place, in aid of the Royal Cambridge Asylum, the bands of the Royal Artillery and Royal Engineers, with the Grenadier, Coldstream and Scots Guards Bands giving their services.

The *Musical Times*, commenting on the concert, says :—

" The Guards Bands in combination did justice to Massenet's *Scènes Pittoresques*. The special successes of the occasion were gained by the string band of the Royal Artillery in the first portion of Schubert's *Unfinished Symphony*, and in the majestic *In Memoriam* overture of Sullivan, the latter a superb performance."

The *British Musician* says :—

" Nothing told better throughout than Sullivan's noble overture *In Memoriam* as rendered by the Royal Artillery Band. Expression and spirit were as near perfection as possible, and the imposing finale made even more than the customary impression upon the hearers."

The R.A. Band, with the bands of the 1st and

2nd Life Guards, Royal Horse Guards, Royal Engineers, Grenadier, Coldstream and Scots Guards, took part in the Grand Military Tattoo at Windsor Castle on the 19th June, 1897. Three days later the band (military) took part in the Diamond Jubilee celebration, and, with the band of the Royal Military School of Music, accompanied Sir George Martin's *Te Deum* at St. Paul's Cathedral. In the evening it played at the family dinner at Buckingham Palace; and also at a garden party there in the following month.

On the 22nd November, 1899, the band, by the gracious command of the late Queen Victoria, gave a State Orchestral Concert in St. George's Hall, Windsor Castle, when the Queen signified her appreciation by presenting Cavaliere Zavertal with a gold-mounted bâton, having on it the Imperial Crown, and embellished with precious stones. His Majesty King Edward VII. and Queen Alexandra (at that time Prince and Princess of Wales), with the Emperor and Empress of Germany, Prince Christian, and many of the nobility, warmly congratulated Cavaliere Zavertal on the performances of the band.

The programme performed on this occasion was :—

1. March ... From the suite "Sylvia" ... ... Delibes
2. Vorspiel ... "Das Heimchen am Herd" ... Goldmark
3. Three Dances from the music to "Henry VIII." ... German
4. { (a) Adagietto from the suite "L'Arlésienne" ... Bizet
   { (b) ... ... "La Chaise à Porteurs" ... Chaminade
5. Ballet Music ... "Der Dämon" ... ... Rubinstein
6. ... ... "Abendruhe" ... ... Loeschhorn
7. Angelus from the suite "Scènes Pittoresques" ...Massenet
8. Overture ... ... "Cleopatra" ... ... Mancinelli
"York Marsch"
"God save the Queen"

In 1900 the band attended Her late Majesty's garden party at Buckingham Palace; and again when the Prince and Princess of Wales received Earl Roberts on his return from the Boer War (1901).

On the 22nd February, 1901, it was ordered to take part in the funeral procession of Her late Majesty Queen Victoria, and had the honour (by His Majesty's command) of being placed in front of the Royal remains, playing Chopin's *Marche Funèbre*, which started the procession.

The band was engaged (both orchestral and military) at the International Exhibition, Glasgow, 1901, from July 29th to August 10th, and had a fine reception, "for nowhere are the Royal Artillery more admired than in the Second City"—(*Glasgow Evening News*). Its performances were highly commented upon, and as "an orchestra it was declared to be the finest combination that had been before the Glasgow public"—(*Orchestral Times*).

In January, 1902, some doubts were expressed in the *Orchestral Times* as to the abilities of the R.A. Band as a military band. The article referred to was :—"It has become the fashion lately in certain circles to acknowledge the high attainments of the Royal Artillery Band as an orchestra, but to assert that as a military band there has been a great falling off during the last decade."

This resulted in some correspondence, and it was then decided, with the approval of the Commander-in-chief, to give a military band performance at one of the London concerts. The first Queen's Hall concert of the year (21st March) was the one

selected. The programme was divided into two
portions, the one orchestral, and the other military.
The programme was :—

ORCHESTRAL.

March	...	"Pomp and Circumstance"	...	Elgar
Symphony	...	"From the New World"	...	Dvořák

MILITARY BAND.

Fest Marsch from "Tannhäuser"	...	...	...	Wagner
Overture in C (op. 24)	...	...	...	Mendelssohn
Scenes from the opera "Una Notte a Firenze"		...	L. Zavertal
Overture	...	...	"Guillaume Tell"	...	...	Rossini

The concert was highly successful, and " reflected
great credit upon Cavaliere Zavertal,[1] and his
accomplished subordinates."

The *Orchestral Times* says :—

" We feel proud in being the acknowledged cause
of this interesting departure, since it was con-
clusively proved that the Royal Artillery Military
Band is in every way worthy of its long reputation,
of its distinguished conductor, and of the noble
regiment to which it belongs."

The *Daily Graphic* says :—

" The idea was a capital one, and gave incon-
testible proof of the versatility of · the Royal
Artillery musicians, who appear to be just as
much at home with clarionets and cornets as with
violins and 'cellos."

The *Standard* says :—

" The subsequent performances yesterday showed

---

[1] " The bandmaster who, above all others that have
played a part at our Exhibition, showed a thorough under-
standing of what music is suitable for a military band, is
Cavaliere Zavertal."—*GlasgowEvening News*.

that the string players were equally at home with the wood wind family, and most effective renderings were secured of the reception music from the second act of *Tannhäuser*, etc."

The *Daily Telegraph* says:—

" The musicians . . . . then came forward as a military band, in which capacity success was again achieved."

The *Daily News* says:—

" A capital military programme was gone through."

The *Daily Chronicle* says:—" The result was highly satisfactory."

The instrumentation of the band on this occasion was:—

MILITARY.

Piccolos	...	2	3rd and 4th Horns...	...	4
Flutes ...	...	2	Althorns ...	...	3
Oboes ...	...	4	Trombones ...	...	5
B flat Clarionets (1st & 2nd)		4	Euphoniums	...	4
1st B flat Clarionets	...	13	Bombardons	...	7
2nd ,, ,,	...	9	Contra Basses (String)	...	2
3rd ,, ,,	...	6	Timpany ...	...	1
Bassoons (1st and 2nd)	...	4	Side Drum ...	...	1
1st Cornets ...	...	7	Bass Drum and Cymbals		1
2nd ,, ...	...	6			—
1st and 2nd Horns ...	...	5			90

ORCHESTRA.

1st Violins ...	...	15	Cornets ...	...	4
2nd ,, ...	...	14	Horns ...	...	4
Violas ...	...	10	Trombones ...	...	4
'Cellos ...	...	9	Euphonium...	...	1
Contra Basses	...	10	Timpany ...	...	1
Harp ...	...	1	Side Drum ...	...	1
Flutes and Piccolo ...	...	3	Bass Drum ...	...	1
Oboes and Cor Anglais	...	3	Cymbals ...	...	1
Clarionets ...	...	3			—
Bassoons ...	...	3			88

The R.A. Band, with the bands of the 1st and 2nd Life Guards, 10th Hussars, R.A. Mounted Band, Royal Engineers, Grenadier, Coldstream, Scots and Irish Guards, Royal Marine Artillery, Royal Marines (Plymouth and Deal), and the Royal Military School of Music, gave a grand military concert at the Crystal Palace on the 9th July, 1901, in aid of the service charities. The R.A. Band also supplied the orchestral accompaniments to many eminent singers, among whom were Miss Macintyre, Miss Marie Brema, Mr. Santley, Mr. Ben Davies, and Signor Ancona.

On the occasion of the Coronation Procession of H.M. King Edward VII., 9th August, 1902, the band (military) was stationed on a specially erected platform opposite the Guards' Memorial in Waterloo Place. It was engaged also during the City of London Coronation Celebration, 25th October, 1902, when the King and Queen were entertained to luncheon at the Guildhall, on which occasion a portion of the band (orchestral) performed during the reception in the Guildhall Library, whilst another portion (military) was stationed on the line of route.

On the following day the band (orchestral) was in attendance at St. Paul's Cathedral when Their Majesties attended the Thanksgiving Service. Here they performed: overture, *Loyal Hearts*, L. Zavertal; Mendelssohn's *Hymn of Praise*; *Ave Maria*, Schubert; and Wagner's *Kaisermarsch*. Sir George Martin's *Te Deum* was also accompanied by the band, and the composer expressed on this, as also on the occasion of the Diamond Jubilee Celebration, his sincere commendation on the artistic rendering of the pieces.

The reputation of the Royal Artillery Band is second to none in the metropolis. It has been engaged at the most important city functions at the Guildhall for many years, notably the receptions given to Prince Albert Victor of Wales, 1885; Shah of Persia, 1889; Emperor of Germany, 1891; King of Denmark, 1893; Khedive of Egypt, 1900; Lord Milner, 1901; Earl Roberts and Viscount Kitchener, 1902; President of the French, 1903; King of Italy, 1903; etc., etc.; and the Lord Mayors' Banquets. It has been in frequent attendance at the receptions, conversaziones, dinners, balls, etc., held at the Mansion House, Foreign Office,[1] Colonial Office, India Office, Royal Academy, etc., and most of the city companies, institutes, societies, etc., and among its patrons may be mentioned the Duke of Sutherland, the Duke of Westminster, the Duchess of St. Albans, the late Marquis of Salisbury, Earl of Londesborough, Lord Wolverton, Lord Brassey, Baron Rothschild, etc.; engaged by the latter during the visit of His Majesty the King (then Prince of Wales) in 1885, and also during the visit of the late Queen Victoria in 1890.

The following programmes are inserted as specimens of the music performed by the Royal Artillery Band at the present time. The first programme is of interest, since it was not performed;

[1] Lord Granville was extremely interested in the R.A. Band, and whilst he was Colonial and Foreign Secretary the band was always engaged at the official functions.

for the Royal Artillery Theatre, where the R.A.
Concerts were held, was totally destroyed by fire
in the early morning of the 18th November, 1903,
the day on which the concert was to have been
given:—

ORCHESTRAL.

ROYAL ARTILLERY CONCERT,

Wednesday, 18th November, 1903.

PART I.

1. Marche du Synode de " Henry VIII." ...   ...   Saint-Saëns

2. Symphony, No. 9 in D dur   ...   .Mozart
Allegro assai, Andante, Allegro

PART II.

3. " Scènes Alsaciennes " (Souvenirs)   ...   ...   Massenet
     i. Dimanche matin
     ii. Au Cabaret
     iii. Sous les Tilleuls
     iv. Dimanche soir

4. Sevillana (Scèna Espagnole)   ...   .   Elgar

5. Quintette (Strings) " Schlummerlied "   ...   L. Zavertal

6. Overture   ...   " Die Moldaunixe "   ...   Rozkosny

ORCHESTRAL.

ROYAL ARTILLERY BAND CONCERT,

Queen's Hall, Langham Place,

December 17th, 1903.

PART I.

1. March   ...   ...   " Cleopatra "   ...   ...   Mancinelli

2. " Symphonie " 2e en la mineur   ...   ...   Saint-Saëns
     i. { *Allegro marcato*
       { *Allegro appassionato*
     ii. *Adagio*
     iii. *Scherzo Presto*
     iv. *Prestissimo*

166

PART II.

3. " Les Erinnyes" (Tragédie Antique) ... ... Massenet
    i. Prélude
    ii. Entr'acte
    iii. Final.

4. "Berçeuse de Jocelyn " ... ... Godard

5. Sevillana (Scène Espagnole) ... ... Elgar

6. Intermezzo ... ... " Cleopatra" ... ... Mancinelli

7. " Capriccio Italien" ... ...Tschaïkowsky

MILITARY BAND.

SUNDAY CONCERTS, ROYAL ALBERT HALL,

28th February, 1904.

ROYAL ARTILLERY MILITARY BAND.

Marche Indienne ... "L'Africaine" ... ... Meyerbeer

From the suite " L'Arlésienne" ... ... Bizet
    i. Prélude.   ii. Minuetto

" Ungarische Tänze," No. 5 ... ... Brahms

Overture ... "William Tell"... ... ... Rossini

Cavaliere Zavertal, the conductor of the R.A. Band, is a prolific composer, and in addition to the opera *Tita*, he has written two others, *Una Notte à Firenze* and *Mirra*.

Una Notte à Firenze (Lorenzaccio), his tragic opera, was composed in 1870, and produced at Prague ten years later, where it excited a perfect *furore* of enthusiasm,[1] and a special performance

[1] *Musical Biography.*—BAPTIE, 1883.

of the opera was given for the Crown Prince
Rudulf of Austria, at his personal request.
Through its interesting action and charming music,
it gained the favour of the critics and public.
Fired by the success of this work and the approval
of the public, he wrote a second opera for the
National Theatre at Prague, called *Mirra*, which was
successfully produced there on the 7th November,
1886, and at the conclusion of the performance
the composer was presented with a wreath of
laurels.

Whilst at Prague, Cavaliere Zavertal made the
acquaintance of Dvořák, and owing to the anta-
gonism of a Wagnerian section the latter said that
he would conduct the opera *Mirra* if no one else
did. When the eminent Bohemian composer visited
England, he was the guest of Cavaliere Zavertal
at Woolwich; and when he heard the R.A. Band
(military) playing the *Church Call* ("Christchurch
Bells")[1] at the Sunday morning church parade,
he remarked, "It sounds like a beautiful organ."
He also attended one of the R.A. Concerts in the
theatre, when the band (orchestral) performed his
new overture *Mein Heim*.

Among innumerable smaller works for orchestra
and military band, including selections, overtures,

---

[1] The "church call" was first played in Woolwich by
the R.A. Bugle Band in the early "sixties," and was also
played by the R.H A. Band during the "seventies." When
this band was broken up in 1878, it was taken up by the
R.A. Band, and has since been played regularly at the
Sunday morning church parade. The notation (as played
by the band) is to be found in *Spare Moments with the Royal
Artillery Band*—BOOSEY & Co., 1889.

M 2

marches, dance music, etc., and many beautiful
songs, which Cavaliere Zavertal has written, we
may mention a quartette for piano, violin, viola,
and 'cello, and an *Album* for the pianoforte, dedicated to Queen Margherite of Italy, who graciously
sent him in return a handsome pin of considerable
value, with her initials cut in diamonds and rubies.

He has also written two symphonies, in which he
" has shown himself to be a master of orchestration
and to possess in a pronounced degree the gift of
musical expression."

His first symphony, in C minor, dedicated to his
father, received high praise from the London and
Dresden Press, and was highly commended by
Dr. Richter, who promised to introduce it to Vienna.

The second, in D minor, was first produced at an
R.A. Concert, April, 1888, and was highly spoken of
in our leading journals. The *Times*, *Daily Telegraph*,
Standard, *Athenæum* and others agreed in declaring
this symphony a masterpiece. From a commendatory notice in the *Athenæum* we quote the
following :—" The themes throughout this symphony are remarkably piquant and spirited, and the
treatment clear and concise, though strictly sym-
phonic. The scoring is very full and rich, the writing
for the wind showing . . . . a full knowledge of the
art of producing true colour and contrast."

" The power of writing melodiously," says the
Musical Times, " is shown in all its movements, in
the *andante* especially, while everywhere the instrumentation is managed with consummate skill."

The *Musical World* says :—" The experienced hand
could be detected in the skilful orchestration."

Cavaliere Zavertal is now a naturalised British subject. and the senior bandmaster in the service. He received his commission as honorary second lieutenant on the 28th December, 1898, which was followed on the 15th November, 1899, by the full rank.

For his services during the Diamond Jubilee Celebration, Queen Victoria bestowed on him the Jubilee Medal, and in March, 1901, His Majesty King Edward VII. decorated him at Marlborough House with the Royal Victorian Order, appointing him a member of the fifth class. He has also received official recognition from several European monarchs. For doing credit to the Italian art in a foreign country, King Humbert nominated him Cavaliere of the Crown of Italy. His Majesty the King of Greece conferred on him the high honour of the Order of the Redeemer. The late King of Servia appointed him a Knight Companion of the Royal Order of Takova, and the Sultan of Turkey bestowed on him the Commander's Star of the Osmaniéh. Some years ago a further distinction, valuable because of its extreme rarity, was conferred on him when the Society of St. Cecilia of Rome elected him one of its members.

On the 26th June, 1896, the Duke of Cambridge, Colonel-in-Chief of the Royal Artillery, visited Woolwich, and decorated Cavaliere Zavertal with the Saxe-Coburg-Ernestine Order of Art and Science, conferred on him by His Royal Highness the Duke of Saxe-Coburg and Gotha. There was a full parade of the Royal Artillery in garrison in honour of the event, when the Duke of Cambridge read the letter which had been received from the Duke of Saxe-Coburg and Gotha[1]:—

"CLARENCE HOUSE, ST. JAMES'S, S.W.,
"30th March, 1896.

"SIR,—I am directed by the Duke of Saxe-Coburg and Gotha to forward to you the Cross of His Royal Highness's Order of Art and Science for presentation to the conductor of the Royal Artillery Band, Cavaliere L. Zavertal. His Royal Highness has had frequent opportunities of hearing the band both at the Albert Hall and the Royal Academy, and he is desirous of showing his great appreciation of the very high state of proficiency the band has been brought to under Cavaliere Zavertal's management by sending him the Order I have named.

"I am desired to request that you will be kind enough to have His Royal Highness's wishes carried out at an early date.

"I have the honour to be, etc.,
"(Signed) D. J. MONSON,
"Comptroller."

The Duke of Cambridge said he was very pleased to have the opportunity of carrying out His Royal Highness's wishes, and, addressing Cavaliere Zavertal, said:—"I can only tell you that the admirable manner in which your band is conducted bears testimony to the great care and talent bestowed upon it. In addition to being yourself gifted, you have the power of instilling into the minds of the various bandsmen the delicacy of

[1] This letter was first made known at the annual ball of the Royal Artillery Band in the R.A. Theatre, when the present Sir Frederick Maurice, K.C.B., then Commandant of Woolwich (who always honoured this function, together with Lady Maurice, by their presence), read the letter to the whole assembly.

..., K.G., decorating Cavaliere L. Zavertal, R.A.,

... ... Ernestine Order for Art and Science,

at Woolwich, 26th June, ...

touch which is required by the players of the various instruments." After a few further complimentary remarks, he concluded by saying that he did not hesitate to declare that the superior of the Royal Artillery Band did not exist in this or in any other country.

To be successful in art, one must be always beating his own record. And in that respect Cavaliere Zavertal stands pre-eminent. He took over the Royal Artillery Band with one hundred and twenty years' reputation as a wind and string band, which has steadily increased as military and orchestral music advanced; yet since he became conductor its reputation has advanced yearly, until it is now acknowledged one of the finest military (wind) bands in British service,[1] and "the finest permanent orchestra in the kingdom"[2]; "whilst the band as a whole will bear comparison with any in the world,"[3] thus worthily sustaining the proud motto of the distinguished regiment to which it belongs—UBIQUE.

---

[1] Although bearing well in mind Mr. Malaprop's legend that "comparisons is oderous," we may be permitted to mention the competition opened by the proprietors of *The Regiment* newspaper in February, 1897, for their readers to decide by vote which were "the six best military (army) bands in the United Kingdom." The result was:—

    1st—Royal Artillery Band
    2nd—Grenadier Guards
    3rd—Royal Engineers
    4th—Coldstream Guards
    5th—Scots Guards
    6th—Royal Marines

[2] *Orchestral Times*, Feb., 1902.

[3] *Referee*, Oct., 1903.

APPENDIX A.

Establishment of the Royal Artillery Band, June, 1904.

1 Bandmaster (2nd lieutenant)
1 Band Sergeant (hon. sergeant-major)
4 Sergeants (1 hon. quartermaster-sergeant)
2 Band Corporals (1 hon. sergeant)
2 Corporals (1 hon. sergeant)
2 Bombardiers (1 hon. sergeant, 1 hon. corporal)
4 Acting Bombardiers (2 hon. sergeants,[1] 1 hon. corporal)
10 Unpaid Acting Bombardiers (3 hon. sergeants)
16 Musicians
51 Bandsmen (gunners)
—
93

Boys' Detachment, R.A. Band.[2]

4 Gunners
10 Boys
—
14

[1] Two honorary sergeants at Kneller Hall, undergoing a course of training for bandmasters.

[2] This detachment comprises men and boys in various stages of proficiency, from which vacancies in the band are filled.

APPENDIX B.

1772—Antony Rocca

1774—Georg Köhler

1777—Friedrich Wielle

1802—G. Schnuphass

1805—M. Eisenherdt

1810—George McKenzie

1845—William G. Collins

1854—James Smyth

1881—Cavaliere Ladislao Zavertal

APPENDIX C.

BAND SERGEANTS
(HONORARY SERGEANT-MAJORS SINCE 1863),
ROYAL ARTILLERY BAND.

1810—John Wilkinson

1837—William Collins (sen.)

1843—Robert Scott

1847—William Newstead (sen.)

1852—Thomas Gilbertson

1853—Samuel Collins

1861—John Parlie

1867—Thomas Butter

1870—Albert Mansfield

1882—John Montara

1889—George Browne

1889—Edward Walker[1]

1896—Walter Sugg[2]

1901—Albert C. Mansfield[3]

[1] Bandmaster of the Honourable Artillery Company.
[2] Musical director, Grand Theatre, Woolwich.
[3] The nephew of Albert Mansfield, the acting bandmaster, R.A., 1880-81.

APPENDIX D.

THE ROYAL HORSE ARTILLERY BAND.

THE first two troops of Royal Horse Artillery were raised in January, 1793, and two drummers, furnished with bugle-horns, were allowed to each troop.[1] About 1797, trumpets were given to them, and they were designated trumpeters.

In the early years of the last century we find that the Royal Horse Artillery possessed a band, and this, although not officially recognised, was the first mounted band in the regiment. It was supported solely by the officers of that branch, and was composed of the trumpeters of the various troops, under the direction of the trumpet-major.

It was not of much importance until the appointment of Bombardier Henry Lawson, of the R.A. Band, as trumpet-major, R.H.A., in succession to Hall. Henry Lawson was one of the finest cornet players of the age, having been compared with Kœnig, the famous cornet player of Jullien's Band.[2] Lawson joined the R.A. Band in 1823, and was the first solo cornet in its ranks. In 1845 he was

---

[1] *History of the R.A.*—DUNCAN, 1872.
[2] *Music and Musicians.*—MARR, 1887.

From a photo.

James H. Browne

appointed ...
tuition ...
was d... ...
the F... ...
positi... ...

Ge... ...
Col... ...
Law... ...
trum... ...
the b... ...
W... ...
to b... ...
p... ...
be... ...
tra... ...
tro... ...
cha... ...

He ...
His ... ...
first an... ...
vacancy ... ...
else.

James ...
Place, V...
essent... ...
sergea... ...
wounded in the lost ...
Buenos Ayres (18...
sergeant in the Royal H... ...
was bandmaster of the 4... ...
half-brother was colour-serge... ...
regiment, and was killed at I.h.r...

From a photo.

appointed trumpet-major, R.H.A., and under his tuition the band made considerable progress. He was discharged in 1852, and became bandmaster of the Forfar and Kincardine Militia Artillery, which position he held until his death in 1856.

George Collins, a brother of the Bandmaster Collins, R.A., was appointed trumpet-major when Lawson was discharged. He was a fine field trumpeter and a fair cornet player, and under him the band was brought to a high state of proficiency. When the organisation of the regiment was changed to brigades in 1859, Collins was appointed alternately to A and B brigades, whichever happened to be stationed at Woolwich. In addition to the trumpeters, two drivers were allowed from each troop or battery for the band. Collins was discharged in January, 1870.

He was succeeded by Sergeant James Alexander Browne, of the R.A. Band, but as bandmaster—the first and only one in the Royal Horse Artillery, the vacancy of trumpet-major being filled by someone else.

James Alexander Browne was born at Artillery Place, Woolwich, 9th May, 1838, and belongs to an essentially military family. His grandfather was a sergeant-major in the 6th Carabineers, and was wounded in the Irish Rebellion (1798) and again at Buenos Ayres (1806). His father was a staff-sergeant in the Royal Horse Artillery; his uncle was bandmaster of the 49th Regiment, and his half-brother was colour-sergeant of the same regiment, and was killed at Inkerman.

In December, 1848, James Browne[1] joined the R.A. Band, being instructed on the flute and violin. But his great ambition was to use his pen; and from mere observation and personal study, without lessons from anyone, he began to compose and arrange, and in November, 1851, when only thirteen years old, a selection from *Norma*, which he had arranged for orchestra, was performed at the R.A. Concerts.

This brought him to notice, and a few years later we find him the solo flautist of the band and playing first violin, at the same time fulfilling engagements in the principal London orchestras.

In 1866 he was sent to Maidstone for six weeks to organise a band for the Royal Horse Artillery Depôt, and in December, 1869, he was offered the bandmastership of the Royal Horse Artillery at Woolwich, and was appointed the following month.

Under his bâton the band attained a degree of skill equal to the best cavalry bands in the service, and about six months after his appointment he was publicly complimented by the late Duke of Cambridge on the improvement of the band.

The reputation of the band increased so rapidly that it fulfilled engagements in all parts of the country. The late Mr. Fred Godfrey thought so well of it that for many years, when the Coldstream Guards Band was unexpectedly ordered for duty, he sent his engagements to the R.H.A. Band.

---

[1] His two younger brothers [George and William] also served in the band, and one of his sons (who was for a time in the band) is at present a battery sergeant-major in the regiment.

As there had been a great increase in the number of batteries. the trumpeters who had not a settled position in the R.H.A. Band were dispensed with altogether, and bandsmen were mustered as non-commissioned officers and drivers.

The band mounted thirty-six men, with kettle-drums and scarlet bannerols. The uniform was similar to that of the rank and file, with the exception of the busby plume, which was scarlet.

After the Franco-Prussian War there was a great increase in our Field Artillery; and in consequence there were two large bands—the R.A. Band and the R.A. Brass Band, both dismounted and without duty; while the R.H.A. Band had to attend all the parades of the Royal Horse Artillery and the Field Artillery. The officers of the former naturally resented this, as they supported the band, and frequently when they required its services found it ordered for duty with the Field Artillery.

This brought matters to a climax, and towards the end of 1877, just as Mr. Browne was getting the band in first-rate order, with apparently a splendid future before them, a committee decided, with the approval of the Duke of Cambridge, on the formation of a Royal Artillery Mounted Band, to be composed of the best members of the R.H.A. Band and the R.A. Brass Band, under Bandmaster James Lawson, of the latter.

Mr. Browne retired as bandmaster on the dissolution of his band, when he accepted the position as bandmaster to the South Metropolitan Schools at Sutton. He has been very successful in this position, having sent some hundreds of boys into army bands, and in 1880 he took first prize at the School Bands Competition at the Crystal Palace. He retired from this position at the dissolution of the Schools (1902).

He was musical director at the Royal Court Theatre, 1880-1, under Mr. Wilson Barrett, and has been conductor of several orchestras. He has written much music, and though very little of it has been published, his selections " From East to West," " Nautical Gems," " Reminiscences of Sir Henry Bishop," etc., issued by Messrs. Lafleur, have been popular for over twenty-five years, and still command a sale.

During the past twenty years he has been engaged in several literary ventures. While serving in the R.A. Band he made a name for himself in the literary world by his *North-West Passage* (1860), and also his *England's Artillerymen* (1865), a historical record of the regiment. He was also engaged by the committee of the Royal Artillery Institution on literary work, and during 1884-5 contributed many articles to the *Service Advertiser*.

He was editor and proprietor of the *Surrey Musical Journal*, 1885-6, sub-editor of the *British Bandsman* from 1891, and sole editor from 1895-98 inclusive; and since 1900 he has been editor of the *Orchestral Times*.

APPENDIX E.

THE ROYAL ARTILLERY MOUNTED BAND
(WOOLWICH).

"THE Corps of Drummers and Fifers," as they delighted in being designated, had existed since 1747, when Colonel Belford introduced "the first fifers in the British Army" into the Royal Artillery (*see* Chap. I.).[1] Exactly a century afterwards the drum was discarded as a signal instrument in the R.A.,[2] but was retained as a marching instrument in conjunction with the fife.

The drums and fifes at Woolwich, under the care of the drum-major and fife-major, was a very efficient band, and relieved the R.A. Band from much regimental duty.

In 1856, with the Crimean War at an end, great changes were made in the organisation of the army.

Sir Fenwick Williams, the Commandant of Woolwich, decided to abolish the drums and fifes in the Artillery, and to introduce in their place a bugle band, using the same service-pattern bugle. The organising and training of this band was entrusted to Trumpet-Major James Lawson, the well-known solo cornet player of the R.A. Band, who, by his indomitable perseverance, raised it

[1] *Memoirs of the R.A.*—MACBEAN.
[2] *Artillery Regimental History.*—MILLER.

N

from "the humble position of a small bugle band to one of the finest military bands in the service."[1]

James Lawson[2] was born at Mill Lane, Woolwich, 11th October, 1826, and came from an old artillery family, his grandfather, father—who was master-gunner at Tilbury Fort, and five brothers all served in the regiment.[3] He joined the R.A. Band in 1839, and was instructed on the B flat clarionet, singing the solo soprano in the band choir, until his seventeenth year. Having some liking for the cornet, the bandmaster placed him under the tuition of his elder brother, Henry, the solo cornet, and such progress did he make that within eighteen months he made his *début* as a soloist at a morning concert in the Officers' Mess, where he was complimented by Lord Bloomfield, who came from among the audience to congratulate him.[4]

Mr. Lawson took Kœnig as his model; his tone was pure, and his execution more like that of a vocalist than a performer on a brass instrument. Firework exhibitions were not to his taste, though he could play florid-tongueing polkas with any of his contemporaries.[5] In 1845 he succeeded his brother as solo cornet, and he now devoted himself to musical study, taking lessons in harmony and composition from John James Haite, of London, a well-known musician and writer of the time. He was appointed fife-major, R.A., and later

[1] *Music and Musicians.*—MARR, 1887.
[2] His grandson is at present serving in the band.
[3] Two of these, Henry and Edward, served in the band.
[4] *Kentish Independent*, 12-1-01.
[5] *Orchestral Times*, Feb., 1903.

Photo by Long & Faulkner, Woolwich.

a small bugle's
in the s...
... in 1859,
t, singing
until his
for the
under the
cornet,
eighteen
morning
was com-
from

his tone
that of a
instrument.
though
with any
... his
himself
... and
London,
the time.
and later

in the band
served in the band.

Photo by Long & Faulkner, Woolwich.

Lawson

trumpet-major, R.A., and in 1856 he was selected
to form the R.A. Bugle Band. He pointed out
to the officers that his men, being restricted to
harmonics of the service instrument, the tunes
would soon become monotonous; so they consented
to let him introduce a chromatic attachment which
fitted to the bugle and gave it practically the same
compass as the cornet.

The band at first numbered only twenty-four
performers, and made its first appearance less than
twelve weeks from its formation at the guard
mounting parade. During the summer evenings of
1857-8 hundreds of people assembled every night at
nine o'clock to hear this band perform the tattoo on
the front parade. In the course of time the band
proved so serviceable that B flat horns, B flat
tenors, euphoniums and basses were introduced;
but all in copper.

The duties in connection with his band were
found to be such that it necessitated Mr. Lawson
severing his connection with the R.A. Band, which
took place in October, 1858. Up to 1859 he held
the position of trumpet-major, R.A., but in this
year the ranks of regimental trumpet-major, drum-
major and fife-major were abolished. It was
decided, however, that Mr. Lawson should be borne
on the establishment of the regiment as drum-
major, and he drew his pay as such, although he
never wielded the drum-major's staff, but was
known as the leader of the bugle band. He was
appointed master on the 1st April, 1865, but
continued to be borne on the pay lists of the
regiment as drum-major until 1882.

Mr. Lawson was now looking ahead to more ambitious performances, and we find that so marked a progress did his band make that he had it entirely re-instrumented as a brass band; and in May, 1869, it was ordered that in future it should be known as "The R.A. Brass Band," numbering forty-seven performers. With this formation it entered the lists at the Crystal Palace Band Contest in 1871 and carried off the first prize of £50.

In November, 1877, it was decided to form a mounted band for the regiment, composed of the best members of the R.A. Brass Band and the Royal Horse Artillery Band, under the direction of Mr. Lawson, of the former, which came into effect 19th January, 1878. It numbered sixty performers, although only forty-two were mounted, being the largest mounted band in the service, and as such has always headed the Lord Mayor's Procession.

The uniform was a dark blue uniform with gilt buttons, scarlet collar and cuffs, which were laced with gold, as also the back of the skirt. Trousers of dark blue, with scarlet stripe, and a head-dress similar to the R.A. Band—the helmet. They wore a white slung belt and cross belt.

In January, 1882, Mr. Lawson was ordered to proceed to Kneller Hall, where he received his certificate as trained bandmaster in compliance with the Horse Guards' order, and was later appointed to the warrant rank.

The mounted band fulfilled engagements in all parts of the country, and gave concerts at the R.A. Theatre in turns with the R.A. Band, and it is believed to have been the only band that played at

this period the entire symphonies of Beethoven,
Haydn, etc., with wind instruments alone. In 1886
it was engaged at the International Exhibition at
Edinburgh, both at the opening and the closing
ceremonies, and created a great impression, being
considered the finest military band present. Sir
James Gowans, the chairman, spoke highly of its
performances, and Mr. Lawson was publicly presented with a gold medal "as a souvenir of his
visit, and the great satisfaction his band had given."
This was the only medal awarded for musical
performances at the exhibition.[1]

No sooner had it returned to Woolwich than its
dissolution was ordered. The Duke of Cambridge
decided to have a Royal Artillery Mounted Band at
Aldershot, and in November, 1886, twenty-eight
members were transferred to Aldershot to form
the *nucleus* of the new band, under the direction of
Mr. Sims, from the Cavalry Depôt, Canterbury.

Mr. Lawson retired on the 16th November, and
on the 22nd, at a general meeting of the officers of
the Royal Artillery in their Mess-room, an elaborate
testimonial was presented to him. It consisted of
a tea and coffee service in sterling silver, including
a large tray suitably inscribed: " In recognition of
his services as bandmaster, Royal Artillery Mounted
Band, and his long and honourable career of over
forty-seven years in the Royal Regiment of
Artillery."

The remaining twenty musicians of the mounted
band at Woolwich struggled on under Sergeant-

---

[1] *Kentish Independent,* 30-10-86.

Major Anderson until 26th August, 1887, when they were finally assured of their fate. Twelve were drafted into the R.A. Band, which was ordered to provide a mounted portion from its own ranks ; others were transferred to the ranks. Sergeant-Major Anderson is now bandmaster of the 3rd Kent R.G. Artillery.

During the band's short existence, over two hundred passed through its ranks, and it furnished solo cornet players to the bands of the three regiments of Foot Guards,[1] notably the well-known soloist of the Grenadiers, Mr. John Williams, now bandmaster of the 2nd Kent R.G. Artillery. Several of the old mounted band entered Kneller Hall and became successful bandmasters. Among them were Mr. J. Manuel Bilton, the present bandmaster of the Royal Horse Guards, Mr. J. S. Dunlop, late Scots Greys, and the late Mr. Shields, 5th Lancers.

On his retirement, Mr. Lawson found scope for his industry and love of music as an instructor of bands in Kent, Surrey and Essex. For forty years he was bandmaster of the North Surrey Schools at Anerley, and during this long tenure of service he furnished some hundreds of musicians for army bands. For some twelve years he was on the Plumstead Vestry, and was three years on the District Board at Charlton. The Woolwich Board of Guardians had him for about seven years, and was their vice-chairman.

He died on the 19th January, 1903, and was buried at Charlton Cemetery.

---

[1] *Music and Musicians.*—MARR, 1887.

APPENDIX F.

REGULATIONS FOR THE GUIDANCE OF THE MASTER,
THE NON-COMMISSIONED OFFICERS, MUSICIANS,
AND BOYS OF THE
ROYAL ARTILLERY BAND, WOOLWICH,
1ST APRIL, 1856.

1. The master of the band is not required when engaged at practice, etc., to attend to other calls for his presence than those conveyed to him from the offices of the Adjutant-General or Commandant.

2. Battalion matters requiring the presence of men of the band are to be so arranged as not to call upon them during the hours of practice.

3. The hours of assembly for practice, whether for the band at large, adult-learners, or boys, will be intimated by the bandmaster to the orderly non-commissioned officer, who will be held responsible that due warning is given to those whose presence at such practice is required.

4. Clean undress uniform is to be worn by the whole of the band when assembled for practice, whether in the forenoon or afternoon.

5. When at practice, the members of the band are expected to pursue the same line of conduct as required from soldiers when on parade, as far as regards attention and respectful behaviour towards the senior present on the occasion, and under no pretence whatever is any individual to leave the practice-room without first obtaining the permission of the master or non-commissioned officer in charge.

6. The additional pay from the band fund is intended to reward merit and talent, and, as an inducement to young

musicians, so to apply themselves to their profession as to become efficient performers. Inattention or misconduct on the part of any member of the band reported by the master and duly investigated, will subject the individual complained of to permanent forfeiture of such additional pay, or to deprivation thereof for a given time, according to the nature of complaint against him.

7. That the bandmaster may be made aware of all orders concerning the band issued from the office of the Adjutant-General or Commandant, the orderly non-commissioned officer will attend daily at the Garrison Orderly Room to copy such orders, and he will be held responsible that they are, as soon after receipt by him as possible, shown to the master that he may give directions for their being carried out.

8. Each member of the band will be held responsible for the preservation of the instrument or instruments, and music or books, in his possession.

9. Attendance at practice with an instrument in such a state as to prevent or retard practice will subject the individual to punishment for neglect of duty and the charges for repairs, unless he shall have previously reported to the bandmaster that the instrument was out of order.

10. The sergeants of the band will attend the afternoon practice of adult-learners and boys, and it is to be clearly understood that all other non-commissioned officers of the band, and all men in receipt of extra pay from the band fund, are liable to be called upon by the master to assist in such instruction.

11. No music or music book, the property of the regiment, is to be taken from the practice-room without the sanction of the bandmaster and the cognizance of the librarian. The librarian will be held responsible that a record is kept of all music, or books of music, taken (with proper permission) from the practice-room, and that the return thereof is duly noted. In case of books or music being brought back in a defaced or damaged state, the librarian will not fail to acquaint the bandmaster thereof,

that he may determine what course to pursue to have such books or music replaced or repaired at the expense of the person to whom they were entrusted.

12. Leave of absence, whether from practice, parade, or roll call, is only to be obtained on application, through the master of the band, or, in his absence, through the senior sergeant.

13. On the admission into hospital, or absence of any member of the band, the non-commissioned officer in charge of his room will cause the instrument and music in his possession, as well as his regimental appointments and necessaries, to be carefully collected and delivered to the orderly non-commissioned officer, who will make out two inventories, one of what the man had in charge belonging to the band and the property of the regiment, and another of the man's regimental appointments and necessaries. The articles included in the first inventory should be handed over to the sergeant appointed for that duty for safe keeping during the man's absence or sickness, and those in the second inventory should be lodged in the quartermaster's store.

In the case of absence or sickness of those permitted to live out of barracks, the orderly non-commissioned officer will be held responsible for collecting, making inventories, and disposing of their instruments, music, appointments, and necessaries, as above directed.

14. The cleanliness and order of the practice-room will rest with the orderly non-commissioned officer, the senior sergeant detailing weekly, by name, the men and boys who are to be employed under the orderly for those duties.

By order of the Band Committee,

CHARLES BINGHAM, Lieut.-Colonel,
Secretary.

By order of the Commandant,

R. K. FREETH, Captain,
For the Brigade-Major.

INDEX.

CORRIGENDA.

PRINTED BY

H. PRYCE AND SON, 33-35, POWIS STREET,

WOOLWICH, S.E.